I0619925

The Hoodoo Handbook

Crafted by James E. Stewart IV

Copyright Year: 2023

Copyright Notice: By James E. Stewart IV. All rights reserved.

The above information forms this copyright notice: Copyright © 2023 James E. Stewart IV

ISBN: 979-8-218-18586-2

CONTENTS

ACKNOWLEDGMENTS

I give great thanks to my Spiritual community, Friends, and Family that have allowed me patience, time, and support to craft this work. I owe eternal gratitude to my Ancestors holding me true to this and allowing me to be the pathway of this handbook to be created.

The Hoodoo Handbook

PREFACE
(*incantation*)

Take this book and make it yours,
'Cause ain't nobody giving cures,
Just hints, and clues,
That you may use,
Like hymns hidden
In rhythms and blues,

May this book stay with you and yours,
Burning the hands of appropriators.
Stolen fruits become bare, and open no doors,
What's pried from inside shall spoil their cores

Magic shall freely flow through thee,
As placed inside you was a key.
Crafted ancestrally,
Designed masterfully,
This is your blood-born divinity.

1 INTRODUCTION

What is Hoodoo? Ask any Black person in America and you have a variety of answers as varied and complex as our collective story. Some elders may shudder at the term and call it "devil work". Some younger generations may claim it their birthright religion. As I presently prepare this book, we are in what can be considered a Hoodoo reclamation or revival period. The name of our ancestral practice has been called many things: Rootwork, Conjure, Juju, Roots, the Work, and sometimes Voodoo (not to be mistaken with the Haitian Vodou, or West African Vodun).

Hoodoo is the spiritual practice of African Americans, forged in the bondage of slavery for the means of Black survival and resistance. Our ancestors brought elements of the Kongo, Bantu, Ewe, Fon, Igbo and many other tribes and nations with them across the Atlantic into the new land, and these elements are traceable in Hoodoo. They forged Hoodoo on plantations to call forth miracles in situations where fate seemed inevitably tragic. Our ancestors made use of the practices of previous African religions, knowings of the plant world, and syncretism within new systems forced up them. Whereas other religions formed in neighboring lands such as Vodou in Haiti, Santeria in Cuba, Candomblé in Brazil, and other African-derived religions synchronized African spirits with Catholic saints; Hoodoos in America found ways to work spirits through Protestantism and in the natural world. Whether veiled by Christianity in pursuit of assimilation as a means of survival or standing in its own framework of our ancestors; Hoodoo is Black in origin, function, and legacy. It encapsulates our spiritual resistance to the racial terrorism of this country, as well as our conquering abilities to defy all odds. Outsiders may see Hoodoo as merely superstitions, but practitioners recognize it as a means of survival. The tools we use altar the forces of life and death, allowing us a closer conversation and walk with God.

The reason I've formed this work into a guided journal is not solely to gatekeep, but to make fishers of men. To widen the eyes of my siblings to the world around us, waking us into remembrance of ourselves. There are elements of our magic that we must learn from trusted elders and community members, and there is space ahead to document those learnings. However, don't be surprised if you have several "aha" moments when working with this book. When spirit delivers the instructions for a working, one can feel like a frenzied mad scientist. Add a dash of salt, a sprinkle of clove, and a tinch of swamp water…and before you know it, you're conjurin like Moses.

Maybe you're something like me and have realized that after many scattered recipes jotted down on sticky notes, in bibles, and in different parts of your phone and computer; it's time to consolidate things into one place. This book doesn't have to be followed in linear fashion. If you receive a revelation about money conjure within a week of having this book, document it. Allow yourself the freedom to let intuition influence your movements, and open to knowledge from trusted community members, elders, and of course ancestors.

The greater function of this handbook is **legacy**.

You may share the insights that come to you with your family line for your future descendants' survival. Giving a familial book to another family member has more weight than ANY Hoodoo book on the market. The only wrong way to use this handbook is to copy information from the internet and reference books, just to fill in empty sections. What I'm trying to stress unto you in this introduction is to not take this handbook lightly. Cherish the words you add to it. However, don't be afraid of it. Your ancestors and spirit guides will push the pen when you're unsure what to add. They will advise you when you need to pause.

Just listen

2 ANCESTRAL NOTES

Where ya peoples from?

The foundation of Hoodoo is ancestry. To bypass this understanding can lead to misalignment. Not all ancestors have the same intentions for us, nor will they show up for every family member in the same ways. However, someone in the spirit realm of your family was cheering for your arrival into the physical realm. And if you've made it this far in life, you still have several folks still looking out for you. This part of the handbook will help you keep track of your findings into your own ancestry and give you some direction if you're just beginning this part of your journey. You don't have to go the genealogy route with your ancestral work as a first step, but it can provide a good working foundation to allow for the spirits themselves to flow into your life. They'll pull your eyes in certain directions. You may unearth entire stories and truths that were once hidden. They may sweetly open roads of opportunities before for you, in exchange for your curiosity. This simple part of your ancestral work may help you recognize ancestors forgotten from your family for generations. This work is not a sprint, nor a marathon. So be easy on yourself as you *wander* through your ancestry.

Beside each family member's name, write their birthday, city of birth, address, occupation(s) if known, and any other findings...

Maternal Lineage

What's your Mother's full name? _____
_____

Birthday _____
City of Birth _____
Address _____
_____

Occupation _____
Extra notes/findings about them _____
_____
_____
_____

Maternal grandmother's full name _____
_____

Birthday _____
City of Birth _____
Address _____
_____

Occupation _____
Extra notes/findings about them _____
_____
_____
_____

Maternal grandfather's full name _____
_____

Birthday _____
City of Birth _____
Address _____
_____

Occupation _____
Extra notes/findings about them _____
_____
_____
_____

Maternal great-grandmother's full name (*your grandma's mother*) _____

_____

Birthday _____

City of Birth _____

Address _____

_____

Occupation _____

Extra notes/findings about them _____

_____

_____

_____

Maternal great-grandfather's full name (*your grandma's father*) _____

_____

Birthday _____

City of Birth _____

Address _____

_____

Occupation _____

Extra notes/findings about them _____

_____

_____

_____

Maternal great-grandmother's full name (*your grandfather's mother*) _____

_____

Birthday _____

City of Birth _____

Address _____

_____

Occupation _____

Extra notes/findings about them _____

_____

_____

_____

Maternal great-grandfather's full name (*your grandfather's father*) _____

_____

Birthday _____

City of Birth _____

Address _____

_____

Occupation _____

Extra notes/findings about them _____

_____

_____

_____

Maternal great-great grandmother's full name (*your mom's, mom's, mom's mom*) _____

_____

Birthday _____

City of Birth _____

Address _____

_____

Occupation _____

Extra notes/findings about them _____

_____

_____

_____

Maternal great-great grandfather's full name (*your mom's, mom's, mom's dad*) _____

_____

Birthday _____

City of Birth _____

Address _____

_____

Occupation _____

Extra notes/findings about them _____

_____

_____

_____

Maternal great-great grandmother's full name (*your mom's, mom's, dad's mom*) _____

Birthday _____

City of Birth _____

Address _____

_____

Occupation _____

Extra notes/findings about them _____

_____

_____

_____

Maternal great-great grandfather's full name (*your mom's, mom's, dad's dad*) _____

Birthday _____

City of Birth _____

Address _____

Occupation _____

Extra notes/findings about them _____

_____

_____

_____

Maternal great-great grandmother's full name (*your mom's, dad's, mom's mom*) _____

Birthday _____

City of Birth _____

Address _____

Occupation _____

Extra notes/findings about them _____

_____

_____

_____

Maternal great-great grandfather's full name (*your mom's, dad's, mom's dad*) _____
_____

Birthday _____
City of Birth _____
Address _____
_____

Occupation _____
Extra notes/findings about them _____
_____
_____
_____

Maternal great-great grandmother's full name (*your mom's, dad's, dad's mom*) _____
_____

Birthday _____
City of Birth _____
Address _____
_____

Occupation _____
Extra notes/findings about them _____
_____
_____
_____

Maternal great-great grandfather's full name (*your mom's, dad's, dad's dad*) _____
_____

Birthday _____
City of Birth _____
Address _____
_____

Occupation _____
Extra notes/findings about them _____
_____
_____
_____

Maternal Aunts

Full Name _____
Birthday _____
City of Birth _____
Address _____

_____
Occupation _____
Extra notes/findings about them _____

_____

_____

_____

Full Name _____
Birthday _____
City of Birth _____
Address _____

_____
Occupation _____
Extra notes/findings about them _____

_____

_____

_____

Full Name _____
Birthday _____
City of Birth _____
Address _____

_____
Occupation _____
Extra notes/findings about them _____

_____

_____

_____

Maternal Great Aunts

Full Name _____

Birthday _____

City of Birth _____

Address _____

_____

Occupation _____

Extra notes/findings about them _____

_____

_____

_____

Full Name _____

Birthday _____

City of Birth _____

Address _____

_____

Occupation _____

Extra notes/findings about them _____

_____

_____

_____

Full Name _____

Birthday _____

City of Birth _____

Address _____

_____

Occupation _____

Extra notes/findings about them _____

_____

_____

_____

Maternal Great Great Aunts

Full Name _____
Birthday _____
City of Birth _____
Address _____
_____
Occupation _____
Extra notes/findings about them _____
_____
_____
_____

Full Name _____
Birthday _____
City of Birth _____
Address _____
_____
Occupation _____
Extra notes/findings about them _____
_____
_____
_____

Full Name _____
Birthday _____
City of Birth _____
Address _____
_____
Occupation _____
Extra notes/findings about them _____
_____
_____
_____

Maternal Uncles

Full Name _____
Birthday _____
City of Birth _____
Address _____
_____
Occupation _____
Extra notes/findings about them _____
_____
_____
_____

Full Name _____
Birthday _____
City of Birth _____
Address _____
_____
Occupation _____
Extra notes/findings about them _____
_____
_____
_____

Full Name _____
Birthday _____
City of Birth _____
Address _____
_____
Occupation _____
Extra notes/findings about them _____
_____
_____
_____

Maternal Great Uncles

Full Name _____
Birthday _____
City of Birth _____
Address _____
_____
Occupation _____
Extra notes/findings about them _____
_____
_____
_____

Full Name _____
Birthday _____
City of Birth _____
Address _____
_____
Occupation _____
Extra notes/findings about them _____
_____
_____
_____

Full Name _____
Birthday _____
City of Birth _____
Address _____
_____
Occupation _____
Extra notes/findings about them _____
_____
_____
_____

Maternal Great Great Uncles

Full Name _____

Birthday _____

City of Birth _____

Address _____

_____

Occupation _____

Extra notes/findings about them _____

_____

_____

_____

Full Name _____

Birthday _____

City of Birth _____

Address _____

_____

Occupation _____

Extra notes/findings about them _____

_____

_____

_____

Full Name _____

Birthday _____

City of Birth _____

Address _____

_____

Occupation _____

Extra notes/findings about them _____

_____

_____

_____

Significant Cousins

Full Name _____

Birthday _____

City of Birth _____

Address _____

_____

Occupation _____

Extra notes/findings about them _____

_____

_____

_____

Full Name _____

Birthday _____

City of Birth _____

Address _____

_____

Occupation _____

Extra notes/findings about them _____

_____

_____

_____

Full Name _____

Birthday _____

City of Birth _____

Address _____

_____

Occupation _____

Extra notes/findings about them _____

_____

_____

_____

Full Name _____
Birthday _____
City of Birth _____
Address _____
_____
Occupation _____
Extra notes/findings about them _____
_____
_____
_____

Full Name _____
Birthday _____
City of Birth _____
Address _____
_____
Occupation _____
Extra notes/findings about them _____
_____
_____
_____

Full Name _____
Birthday _____
City of Birth _____
Address _____
_____
Occupation _____
Extra notes/findings about them _____
_____
_____
_____

Paternal Lineage

What's your Fathers full name? _____

_____

Birthday _____

City of Birth _____

Address _____

_____

Occupation _____

Extra notes/findings about them _____

_____

_____

_____

Paternal Grandmother's full name _____

_____

Birthday _____

City of Birth _____

Address _____

_____

Occupation _____

Extra notes/findings about them _____

_____

_____

_____

Paternal Grandfather's full name _____

_____

Birthday _____

City of Birth _____

Address _____

_____

Occupation _____

Extra notes/findings about them _____

_____

_____

_____

Paternal great-grandmother's full name (*your grandma's mother*) _____

_____

Birthday _____

City of Birth _____

Address _____

_____

Occupation _____

Extra notes/findings about them _____

_____

_____

_____

Paternal great-grandfather's full name (*your grandma's father*) _____

_____

Birthday _____

City of Birth _____

Address _____

_____

Occupation _____

Extra notes/findings about them _____

_____

_____

_____

Paternal great-grandmother's full name (*your grandfather's mother*) _____

_____

Birthday _____

City of Birth _____

Address _____

_____

Occupation _____

Extra notes/findings about them _____

_____

_____

_____

Paternal great-grandfather's full name (*your grandfather's father*) _____

_____

Birthday _____
City of Birth _____
Address _____

_____

Occupation _____
Extra notes/findings about them _____

_____

_____

_____

Paternal great-great grandmother's full name (*your dad's, mom's, mom's mom*) _____

_____

Birthday _____
City of Birth _____
Address _____

_____

Occupation _____
Extra notes/findings about them _____

_____

_____

_____

Paternal great-great grandfather's full name (*your dad's, mom's, mom's dad*) _____

_____

Birthday _____
City of Birth _____
Address _____

_____

Occupation _____
Extra notes/findings about them _____

_____

_____

_____

Paternal great-great grandmother's full name (*your dad's, mom's, dad's mom*) _____
_____

Birthday _____
City of Birth _____
Address _____
_____

Occupation _____
Extra notes/findings about them _____
_____
_____
_____

Paternal great-great grandfather's full name (*your dad's, mom's, dad's dad*) _____
_____

Birthday _____
City of Birth _____
Address _____
_____

Occupation _____
Extra notes/findings about them _____
_____
_____
_____

Paternal great-great grandmother's full name (*your dad's, dad's, mom's mom*) _____
_____

Birthday _____
City of Birth _____
Address _____
_____

Occupation _____
Extra notes/findings about them _____
_____
_____
_____

Paternal great-great grandfather's full name (*your dad's, dad's, mom's dad*) _____

Birthday _____

City of Birth _____

Address _____

_____

Occupation _____

Extra notes/findings about them _____

_____

_____

_____

_____

Paternal great-great grandmother's full name (*your dad's, dad's, dad's mom*) _____

Birthday _____

City of Birth _____

Address _____

_____

Occupation _____

Extra notes/findings about them _____

_____

_____

_____

_____

Paternal great-great grandfather's full name (*your dad's, dad's, dad's dad*) _____

Birthday _____

City of Birth _____

Address _____

_____

Occupation _____

Extra notes/findings about them _____

_____

_____

_____

Paternal Aunts

Full Name _____
Birthday _____
City of Birth _____
Address _____
_____
Occupation _____
Extra notes/findings about them _____
_____
_____
_____

Full Name _____
Birthday _____
City of Birth _____
Address _____
_____
Occupation _____
Extra notes/findings about them _____
_____
_____
_____

Full Name _____
Birthday _____
City of Birth _____
Address _____
_____
Occupation _____
Extra notes/findings about them _____
_____
_____
_____

Paternal Great Aunts

Full Name _____
Birthday _____
City of Birth _____
Address _____
_____
Occupation _____
Extra notes/findings about them _____
_____
_____
_____

Full Name _____
Birthday _____
City of Birth _____
Address _____
_____
Occupation _____
Extra notes/findings about them _____
_____
_____
_____

Full Name _____
Birthday _____
City of Birth _____
Address _____
_____
Occupation _____
Extra notes/findings about them _____
_____
_____
_____

Paternal Great Great Aunts

Full Name _____
Birthday _____
City of Birth _____
Address _____
_____
Occupation _____
Extra notes/findings about them _____
_____
_____
_____

Full Name _____
Birthday _____
City of Birth _____
Address _____
_____
Occupation _____
Extra notes/findings about them _____
_____
_____
_____

Full Name _____
Birthday _____
City of Birth _____
Address _____
_____
Occupation _____
Extra notes/findings about them _____
_____
_____
_____

Paternal Uncles

Full Name _____
Birthday _____
City of Birth _____
Address _____
_____
Occupation _____
Extra notes/findings about them _____
_____
_____
_____

Full Name _____
Birthday _____
City of Birth _____
Address _____
_____
Occupation _____
Extra notes/findings about them _____
_____
_____
_____

Full Name _____
Birthday _____
City of Birth _____
Address _____
_____
Occupation _____
Extra notes/findings about them _____
_____
_____
_____

Paternal Great Uncles

Full Name _____

Birthday _____

City of Birth _____

Address _____

_____

Occupation _____

Extra notes/findings about them _____

_____

_____

_____

Full Name _____

Birthday _____

City of Birth _____

Address _____

_____

Occupation _____

Extra notes/findings about them _____

_____

_____

_____

Full Name _____

Birthday _____

City of Birth _____

Address _____

_____

Occupation _____

Extra notes/findings about them _____

_____

_____

_____

Paternal Great Great Uncles

Full Name _____
Birthday _____
City of Birth _____
Address _____
_____
Occupation _____
Extra notes/findings about them _____
_____
_____
_____

Full Name _____
Birthday _____
City of Birth _____
Address _____
_____
Occupation _____
Extra notes/findings about them _____
_____
_____
_____

Full Name _____
Birthday _____
City of Birth _____
Address _____
_____
Occupation _____
Extra notes/findings about them _____
_____
_____
_____

Significant Cousins

Full Name _____

Birthday _____

City of Birth _____

Address _____

_____

Occupation _____

Extra notes/findings about them _____

_____

_____

_____

Full Name _____

Birthday _____

City of Birth _____

Address _____

_____

Occupation _____

Extra notes/findings about them _____

_____

_____

_____

Full Name _____

Birthday _____

City of Birth _____

Address _____

_____

Occupation _____

Extra notes/findings about them _____

_____

_____

_____

Full Name _____

Birthday _____

City of Birth _____

Address _____

_____

Occupation _____

Extra notes/findings about them _____

_____

_____

_____

Full Name _____

Birthday _____

City of Birth _____

Address _____

_____

Occupation _____

Extra notes/findings about them _____

_____

_____

_____

Full Name _____

Birthday _____

City of Birth _____

Address _____

_____

Occupation _____

Extra notes/findings about them _____

_____

_____

_____

3 ANCESTRAL GIFTS

Nothing is new under the sun, and apples don't fall too far from their trees. As we grow and become more of ourselves, we may discover that we are inclined to do things that have been done in the family. Whether that be a pursuit of public speaking, a flair for fashion and style, or the ability to read someone for filth with ease; these gifts and abilities vary. They will fluctuate from person to person, identifying our place in the world and the story of our family. Gifts can be nurtured, but the function will tell a story of its own all the way from dormancy to recognition, to its masterful peak in the story of our lives.

It is critical for each of us to actualize our gifts in this lifetime, and when possible, the gifts of others. Perhaps, on the bargaining table for free will, God gave each of us the option to rise to the occasion of our gifts and callings or sit back and let life drift by.

Fear of flying will never taste more bitter than the eternal "what if?"

What common gifts do you notice passed down through your family? Additional pages can be found on page 239

Spiritual Gifts

Spiritual gifts can include powers like dreaming true (*prophecy*), knowing (*various types of precognition*), speaking to fire (*healing burns*), mediumship (*communing with the dead*), conjuration (*magic & spells*), and many others. Upon recognition of a spiritual gift, one should often seek council and mentorship. In families where these gifts may be feared, practitioners should request God and their ancestors to supply a mentor who can nurture these gifts in safe ways. For documentation of spiritual gifts in the spaces ahead, be aware of family members that may use coded language when speaking of spiritual gifts. Ask questions but be mindful and respectful of the comfort levels of elders and family members when broaching this subject.

Spiritual Gift _____

Ancestors Known of possessing said gift _____

_____

_____

_____

Signs/Symptoms of gift awakening _____

_____

_____

_____

Ways to nurture/grow it _____

_____

_____

Pitfalls to avoid _____

_____

_____

Taboos _____

_____

_____

_____

Descendants known of possessing said gift _____

_____

_____

Physical Gifts

As we come to find our way in our bodies, the genetic stories of our families begin to shine through. Some of us come from families of singers, dancers, musicians, athletes, chefs, hairstylists, carpenters, firefighters, teachers, and more. A profession is not a gift, yet it requires one to excel. Identifying professions that your family commonly held and excelled in will spell out the gifts underneath those careers. Gifts of strength, power, precision, rhythm, resilience, gentleness, softness, flexibility, and many others will grow up through us and help decide how we navigate the world. This section is important for you and future generations that may at times find themselves lost in the world, in search of a map of potential ways forward when life gives us its many redirections.

Profession _____

Recognized Gifts _____

_____

Ancestors possessing said gifts _____

_____

_____

Ways to nurture/grow it _____

_____

_____

Pitfalls to avoid _____

_____

_____

Health concerns/advice _____

_____

_____

_____

Descendants known of possessing said gifts _____

_____

_____

_____

Mental Gifts

The gifts that can tie both physical and spiritual ones together are gifts of the mind. Our wit, charm, intellect, humor, cunningness, affability, tenderness, intensity, and other qualities shape our personalities and color our other gifts. When you think of certain branches of your family, you'll think of common traits.

"Oh, the Jones side of the family; they stay crackin jokes."

"Let me tell you about them Jacksons on your momma's side; sharp as a tact, and smart as hell. "

The mental gifts of our families remind us of the different types of intelligences and wisdoms within our culture. Highlighting these gifts in those around you will naturally allow you to know yourself with more clarity and awareness. Recognizing mental gifts will also serve you in creating connections with ancestors you're unfamiliar with. You'll feel the familiar warmth of a known elder's humor. Or the well-known iciness of the stern wit of aunts from a certain line. They'll be glad to see these gifts carried on through you.

Recognized Gift _____
Ancestors possessing said gift _____
_____
_____

Ways to nurture/grow it _____
_____
_____

Pitfalls to avoid _____
_____
_____

Health concerns/advice _____
_____
_____
_____

Descendants known of possessing said gift _____
_____
_____
_____

4 INITIATIONS & KNOWN RITES OF PASSAGE

Initiations mark the movement from one defined aspect of life to another. There are tests that must be passed. Information that will be bestowed. And doors that only Spirits can open to the initiate. These initiations exist in Hoodoo. These have been documented by writers like Zora Neal Hurston, Katrina Hazzard-Donald, Albert J. Raboteau and many others. Initiations are often far more private, secretive, and only shared on a need-to-know basis, even within families. If you choose to document initiations in the sections ahead, heed any warnings from ancestors, spirit guides, and elders that may advise against written documentation of certain or total aspects. From its inception, so much of our practice has been steeped in secrecy. And necessarily so.

Rites of passage often can be more open and frequently communal. Like the first time a younger family member cooks for a major holiday, a baptism, or sacred gift bestowed to a family member on a significant birthday. Knowing the deeper meaning of these rites is important, as we must continue them to ensure proper growth from generation to generation.

For folks creating new pathways in their family lineages, it's more than possible, and quite important to create your own rites of passage for your family or cease or alter ones that are harmful for the family.

In the spaces ahead, document initiations and rites of passage your family may uphold, or ones you intend to create within your family unit. Additional pages can be found on page 239

The name of the initiation/rite _____
_____
_____

Its function/meaning _____
_____
_____
_____

What family member(s) conduct it? _____
_____
_____

When it is time to perform this rite (*requirements*)? _____
_____
_____

Accompanied Tests _____
_____
_____
_____
_____

Associated Ancestors/Spirits _____
_____
_____
_____

Status achieved afterwards _____
_____
_____
_____
_____

5 PLACES OF WORSHIP & RELIGIOUS AFFILIATIONS

Hoodoo gave birth to the Black Church. Its origins are steeped in African traditions, some of which are still recognizable to this day. Although modern relations between the church and Hoodoo may be tepid at best, we are kin. No amount of church hurt or trauma disinherit you from the pathways that you're born from. You may not even claim Christianity, but you still have access to the ways in which your ancestors utilize it in this practice.

Temples, Churches, Mosques, and all places of worship that are affiliated with your family are important to document and know. They weave critical fabrics into our spiritual stories. They color the relationship and lens through which we may see the Creator. Even if you didn't personally attend the place of worship, knowing where a loved one attended will serve you in your ancestral work. Many elders can often remember the point at which the family entered religious observation in the iteration you were born into it. Often, church records will contain critical information for Black families on genealogical pursuits. There may be a story behind a Grandparent joining a church. There may be customs and traditions that sewn inside that you mustn't discard. And there may have been prayers and sacrifices made on your family's behalf in that place of worship; so it will serve you as a place of power.

Note any places of worship affiliated with your family in the pages ahead. Additional pages can be found on page 239

Name of place of worship _____

_____

Address _____

_____

_____

Family Member(s) that attended _____

_____

_____

Time frame they attended _____

_____

_____

Their role in the place of worship _____

_____

_____

Customs & Traditions _____

_____

_____

_____

Any additional notes/findings _____

_____

_____

_____

_____

_____

_____

6 FAMILIAL CURSES

The definition of a generational curse may vary from a behavioral issue that is passed down, or an actual formalized curse that has been placed on a bloodline. It is important to identify the source and type of curse afflicting a family. Divination can reveal the type of curse and what steps need to be taken to alleviate and remove it. Some curses may require divination of someone outside the family, or outside of the afflicted bloodline. Be mindful, not all curses can be lifted with a simple candle lighting or a prayer. Some curses may require dedicated work to lift, but it can be done. Sometimes success and triumph against a curse may be witnessed on an individual level, or entirely throughout the family. Any progress should be lauded, as it can show the way for other family members to free themselves. This section is for practitioners to identify any curses that may lie within their family, and all progression in the work to remove them.

What known ancestral curses exist in your family? Note your findings in the pages ahead.
Additional pages can be found on page 239

Spiritual

In its heyday of the 1800's and the turn of the century, Hoodoo practitioners were known to place roots on enemies that affected entire families. If a transgression was not paid and remedied by the transgressor, it would rattle through a family. In some cases, all family members with a specific surname would be affected. In some cases, anyone of blood relation would be affected. These curses can vary from blockages in a persons life, to a spirit set in motion to plague its targets. Uncovering its origins can reveal keys to break its hold. Just remember, if you are afflicted, you may be blind or partial to seeing all elements at play. Seeking divination from an outside source can be helpful in this process.

Type of curse _____

_____

Divination notes on this curse _____

_____

_____

_____

_____

_____

Family line/Members afflicted _____

_____

_____

_____

_____

_____

Symptoms and attributes of curse _____

_____

_____

_____

_____

Origin of curse (*if known*) _____

_____

_____
_____
_____
_____
_____

Prescription or Remedies suggested _____
_____
_____
_____
_____
_____

Success stories against curse *(this can include individual achievements, or entire familial triumphs)*

_____
_____
_____
_____
_____
_____
_____
_____
_____
_____
_____
_____
_____
_____
_____
_____
_____
_____
_____
_____
_____

Health

Many genetic health concerns have been referred to as curses, but it doesn't necessarily make it true. The famous Conjure Doctor Jim Jordan miraculously healed thousands of people in his time yet was known to turn several clients to health care professionals in matters that needed to be handled medically. One of the largest tell tell signs of a health-related curse is when medical doctors cannot find a cause for the issue, and it seems to be evasive. If all the men on one side of the family pass away at a certain age (or age range), or if the first pregnancy is always a stillborn for a certain line, are examples of possible health-related curses. Be cautious and avoid describing differently abled bodies as cursed. Many monikers of spiritual gifts, talents, and spiritual involvement are labeled as birth defects.

Type of curse _____

_____

Divination notes on this curse _____

_____

_____

_____

_____

_____

Family line/Members afflicted _____

_____

_____

_____

_____

_____

Symptoms and attributes of curse _____

_____

_____

_____

_____

_____

Origin of curse (*if known*) _____

_____
_____
_____
_____
_____
_____

Prescription or Remedies suggested _____
_____
_____
_____
_____
_____

Success stories against curse *(this can include individual achievements, or entire familial triumphs)*
_____
_____
_____
_____
_____
_____
_____
_____
_____
_____
_____
_____
_____
_____
_____
_____
_____
_____
_____
_____
_____
_____
_____

Behavioral

This category of curses is often debatable, as some will classify this as just someone's general disposition that should change. While this may have some truth, certain behaviors replay throughout families, leaving the family to indeed feel cursed. Behaviors such as abandonment, fear of success, apathy, anger, self-harm, and many others can echo into descendant's lives disrupting and upending all sorts of development. In this regard, mental health professionals may at times be the prescription or remedy to recognize and allow space for this curse to be disrupted and cease its hold on a family. Spiritual and medical help can be paired in ones healing journey,

Type of curse _____
_____

Divination notes on this curse _____
_____
_____
_____
_____
_____

Family line/Members afflicted _____
_____
_____
_____
_____
_____

Symptoms and attributes of curse _____
_____
_____
_____
_____
_____

Origin of curse (*if known*) _____
_____
_____

_____
_____
_____

Prescription or Remedies suggested _____
_____
_____
_____
_____

Success stories against curse *(this can include individual achievements, or entire familial triumphs)*
_____
_____
_____
_____
_____
_____
_____
_____
_____
_____
_____
_____
_____
_____
_____
_____
_____
_____
_____

7 ANCESTRAL GRAVEYARDS & CEMETERIES

This section is to document graveyards, cemeteries, and resting sites attributed to your family. There is a section on page 467 to document your ritual and conjuring work within graveyard/cemeteries.

For Black Americans to know where your ancestors are buried is a privilege, we must not take for granted. Even in death, we aren't afforded the same rights and respect as the rest of the country. Knowing the burial sites of loved ones is extremely important in Hoodoo. Altars are the secondary place to leave offerings for our dead, but the burial site is the first and most effective place. Final resting sites are not always in graveyards or cemeteries, or even underground in the case of cremations. Knowing the burial sites of loved ones is essential when doing any graveyard/cemetery work. Ideally, these are the first spirits and places you should work with. Should you begin cemetery work filled with spirits unfamiliar to you, they may not be as forgiving if you make a mistake in your work.

In the sections ahead, document the burial locations of your ancestors. Additional pages can be found on page 239

Name of Ancestor(s) _____
Burial Location _____
Address _____

_____
Cardinal Direction of burial _____
Note any pages of cross references for this ancestor(s) _____

_____

_____

Name of Ancestor(s) _____
Burial Location _____
Address _____

_____
Cardinal Direction of burial _____
Note any pages of cross references for this ancestor(s) _____

_____

_____

Name of Ancestor(s) _____
Burial Location _____
Address _____

_____
Cardinal Direction of burial _____
Note any pages of cross references for this ancestor(s) _____

_____

_____

Name of Ancestor(s) _____
Burial Location _____
Address _____

_____
Cardinal Direction of burial _____
Note any pages of cross references for this ancestor(s) _____

_____

_____

8 LAND/HOUSES/APARTMENTS

Land and home ownership by Black Americans has always been under threat since emancipation and for freed people prior. Having land, houses, or even rent controlled apartments within your family is an inheritance that should be guarded and cherished. Even if you don't live on the land, if you have access to it, this land is a part of your ancestral story. Everything from the dirts, plants, and found materials can be incorporated into your workings. The spirits of every land and home should be acknowledged and documented when possible. Not only the spirits of your family, but ones that may have inhabited these spaces prior.

With the acknowledgement of spirits of the land or home, be aware that certain offerings, rituals, or acts may need to be carried out to ensure that land is protected and remains in the family. When land or homes are lost, it is not a punishment, but a reminder of the dangerous surrounding greed that seeks to pry and exploit us.

In the spaces ahead, document all significant land, houses, and apartments attributed to your family.
Additional pages can be found on page 239

Address _____

_____

_____

Date of ownership _____

Is it still in the family? _____

If not, who presently owns it? _____

Is it accessible? _____

Recognizable spirits _____
_____
_____

Notable plants _____
_____
_____
_____

Homes/Buildings _____
_____
_____

Waters _____
_____
_____

Materials & Other resources _____
_____
_____

Additional notes/findings _____
_____
_____
_____
_____

9 SCRIPTURES, SONGS, DANCES, PRAYERS & POEMS

The expressions of a Black artist can create entire realities with the stroke of a pen. Behind each letter, rhythmic note, and body movement is a spirit guiding the birth of a new thing. When these expressions (doorways) are folded back into our spiritual work, it colors our world a different hue, allowing us a brief touch with heaven. Imagining something a bit better than what may presented before us.

Incorporating your Grandpa's favorite scripture for wisdom, your Auntie's song she loved to shimmy to, or common prayers in your family can be more powerful in your work than anything you find in a Hoodoo Psalm reference book. Why? Because it resonates with your spirit and your family's spirits. Adding arbitrary elements to your work may not always be as effective (especially early in your journey). Working with what is sonically and culturally familiar will be more potent.

One key of Hoodoo is understanding the resonant meaning of a thing, so if (and when) that material thing is unavailable, the understood resonance persists.

Use this section to journal any scriptures, songs, and prayers used in your family or ones you favor. Note their meaning to you. Additional pages can be found on page 239

Scriptures

Many Hoodoo folk use the bible in their workings, but not all do. The bible has its own mysticism observed by Christians, Hebrews, and many occultists. The best way to use it in your Hoodoo is in a way that incorporates your ancestors. In this way, lean on any biblical sharing's from your elders and notes left in family bibles. This will also help make space for you to glean your own understandings of the text from Spirit, instead of only seeing it in a linear doctrine fashion. If your family utilized other sacred texts such as the Torah or Quran, include your findings in the section ahead. You can use this section to write verses, their uses, and meanings to you in your work.

Verse _____
Ancestor or Elder affiliation _____
_____
Interpretation _____
_____
_____
Uses _____
_____
_____
_____

Verse _____
Ancestor or Elder affiliation _____
_____
Interpretation _____
_____
_____
Uses _____
_____
_____
_____

Verse _____
Ancestor or Elder affiliation _____
_____
Interpretation _____
_____

Uses _____
_____
_____
_____

Verse _____
Ancestor or Elder affiliation _____

Interpretation _____
_____
_____

Uses _____
_____
_____

Verse _____
Ancestor or Elder affiliation _____

Interpretation _____
_____
_____

Uses _____
_____
_____

Verse _____
Ancestor or Elder affiliation _____

Interpretation _____
_____
_____

Uses _____
_____
_____

Songs

Our ancestral songs have the ability to break chains, move mountains, and disrupt entire realities around us. Spirits can be called down, called forth, and called up all from a simple hum. As Hoodoo's, we can never underestimate the power of music. Playing music while doing a working can enhance its manifestation, raising not only the energy of your atmosphere, your spiritual team, but also your personal power. Having songs your ancestors loved can help in the conjuration and calling of them. Having songs you personally love will help in focusing your energy. Explore with music you already know, one's your elders favored, ones you find listed in obituaries, and more in the spaces ahead

Song _____

Artists _____

Interpretation _____

_____

_____

Uses _____

_____

_____

Ancestors or spirits affiliated _____

_____

_____

Song _____

Artists _____

Interpretation _____

_____

_____

Uses _____

_____

_____

Ancestors or spirits affiliated _____

_____

_____

Song _____

Artists _____

Interpretation _____

_____

_____

Uses _____

_____

_____

Ancestors or spirits affiliated _____

_____

_____

Song _____

Artists _____

Interpretation _____

_____

_____

Uses _____

_____

_____

Ancestors or spirits affiliated _____

_____

_____

Song _____

Artists _____

Interpretation _____

_____

_____

Uses _____

_____

_____

Ancestors or spirits affiliated _____

_____

_____

Dances

The muscle memories of our sacred dances find their way back to us through both teachers and natural responses to certain rhythms. The isolating of hips, arms flowing like water, and the rocking of heads when specific beats flow through our bodies is ancestral. Our dances tell stories, capture time and sentiment, and can allow for the expression of Spirit into the physical world. Spirits can be recognized during trance and possession by certain movements. Running in certain patterns, hand waves, head jerks, and the buckling of knees tell can tell what spirit may have descended upon the body of a dancer.

As nothing is new under the sun, even the dances of new generations often have recognizable ancestral roots. Some dances link specific regions of the country, others tie families together, and some dances are just part of being Black any and everywhere. Dances can activate spirits of prophecy, war, victory, renewal, and less we forget passion. In the spaces ahead, note dances you recognize in your practice with spiritual significance

Name or Style of dance _____

Origin/Originator _____

_____

Place of origin _____

_____

Era of origin _____

_____

Meaning _____

_____

_____

Themes _____

_____

_____

Notable movements _____

_____

_____

_____

Associated Spirits _____

_____

Spiritual significance _____
_____
_____

Prayers

Prayer, in its simplest form, is a conversation with the divine. Prayers can be elaborate pleas encompassing all the troubles of the heart, or a simple sigh and a cry to the Creator. Little is required of the devotee for activation of prayer other than present moment faith. Sometimes common prayers, prayer structures, or prayer tools and artifacts are shared amongst families. Think about prayers said by elders at family functions. Within them, is there a recognition of God for past victories in relation to what is being requested currently? Are there commonly asked requests of God? And are these requests phrased in a certain manner? These prayer structures change depending on whom is being prayed to, and what is being asked. Document some common prayers in your family, and ones you've added to your practice.

Name of prayer _____

Full Prayer _____

_____

_____

_____

_____

_____

_____

_____

_____

_____

Ancestors or Spirits affiliated _____

_____

_____

_____

Effect or use _____

_____

_____

_____

Origin of prayer (if known) _____

_____

_____

Number of times prayer is to be recited _____

Poems

Poems can store wisdoms needed to pass down to future generations. They can be a written emotional snapshot of a time that breathes life into a person you never met or revealing an entire other side of someone you only knew one dimension of. Whether it was written by an ancestor, or noted as their favorite poem, the words that resonate with an ancestor can connect with them. Not necessarily an incantation, but poems can help call a spirit into place. Jot down some favorite poems of your ancestors/elders below

Name of Poem _____

Author _____

Date Written _____

Full Poem _____

_____

_____

_____

_____

_____

_____

_____

_____

Ancestors or Spirits affiliated _____

_____

_____

Effect, use, or meaning _____

_____

_____

_____

"Mama used to say…"

Did you have a running joke with one of your Uncles? Or did your grandma have a catchphrase when hanging up the phone? Hold on to these phrases. There may be unique wisdoms embedded within, that must be shared down the family line. These sayings can also help spark a connection with an ancestor. Randomly hearing a phrase that only your cousin would say waft from a car radio might not be so random when it serves as an answer to a troubling issue.

Ancestor/Elder _____

Phrase _____
_____
_____

Effect, use, or meaning _____
_____
_____

Ancestor/Elder _____

Phrase _____
_____
_____

Effect, use, or meaning _____
_____
_____

Ancestor/Elder _____

Phrase _____
_____
_____

Effect, use, or meaning _____
_____
_____

Ancestor/Elder _____

Phrase _____
_____
_____

Effect, use, or meaning _____

_____

_____

Ancestor/Elder _____

Phrase _____

_____

Effect, use, or meaning _____

_____

_____

Ancestor/Elder _____

Phrase _____

_____

Effect, use, or meaning _____

_____

_____

Ancestor/Elder _____

Phrase _____

_____

Effect, use, or meaning _____

_____

_____

Ancestor/Elder _____

Phrase _____

_____

Effect, use, or meaning _____

_____

_____

10 HOLY DAYS/CELEBRATIONS

As Black people in America, we decide what holidays will actually mean for us. Because so much of our time and life in this country has been exploited, our rest is sacred. We may not observe Thanksgiving the same way the rest of the country does, nor acknowledge President's day as intended, but we'll take the time off as we damn well should. The holiday, holy days, and tender celebrations we do observe and the way we observe them are cherished. Stories echo down generations of the time Great Aunt Sue joined in the electric slide after years of being sick and bedridden. And you still have the scar from the time you skinned your knee on Uncle Kirks driveway at the family reunion. These points of communion tie us together, and the warmth of our closeness nourishes our ancestors.

There are days we all traditionally observe and have rituals to pair with the occasion (*such as New Year eve/day*), days we personally or within certain lineages pair rituals with (*such as Easter*) and Holidays or months of observance that are newer, yet still sacred (*such as Hoodoo Heritage Month*).

In the spaces ahead, note holy days the way you observe them, any traditions you uphold, or ones you seek to begin and carry on. Additional pages will be found on page 239

Holy Day/Celebration _____

Date observed _____

Date of origin _____

Story of origin/Significance _____

_____

_____

_____

Attributed Spirits _____

_____

Attributed Ancestors _____

_____

Attributed Foods _____

_____

_____

Attributed Music _____

_____

_____

Attributed Dances _____

_____

Attributed Prayers _____

_____

_____

Attributed Rituals _____

_____

_____

_____

_____

_____

_____

_____

11 DIVINATION

The burst of energy that starts as a tingle, flowing to a full-on revelation. A sense. A vision. A knowing. A kin to the high a preacher feels before losing themselves to the Holy Spirit, a diviner steps out of their own way to allow the flow of a message. When the highly structured material world no longer provides a sought-after answer, a querent turns to a diviner. In this fluid, multilayered world, messages can be complex and simple at the same time. A Hoodoo diviner may use cards, bones, bibliomancy, water, fire, or a wide variety of tools and forms to tap into the spiritual realm and seek guidance. Each process is unique and personalized to every diviner. While reading for others may not be your calling, each of us possesses the ability to divine on a situation. Divination is an important step in all Hoodoo workings, as we must discern the necessity before taking action. This section will allow space for you to write your process or carve it out if you're looking for ways to begin.

In the pages ahead, note your knowings & findings in this realm. For the "Tools I use" section, there are 54 prompts for describing the pieces you use in your divination work. There may be more or fewer pieces in your system of divination. Additional pages can be found on page 239

Tools I use

What are your preferred ways of reading? Tarot? Playing Cards? Bones? The Bible? Fire? Water? Other? This may grow and adapt over time, depending on the situation you're divining on, your mood, or your status in your spiritual community. In the spaces ahead, use whichever depictions apply to note various meaning, interpretations, and revelations you have within that divination style. Certain styles of divination will require you to first learn the intended meaning of each piece of the system. You can include that in the spaces here, but please don't stop there. Remain open to how different messages can be conveyed through your tools.

Tool _____

Author/creator (*if known*) _____

Mainly used for these types of readings_____

_____

_____

How to prepare a reading _____

_____

_____

_____

Various spreads or styles _____

_____

_____

_____

Spirits traditionally called on with this tool _____

_____

How to close/end a reading _____

_____

_____

_____

Ways to cleanse, or refresh tools _____

_____

_____

_____

_____

Number of pieces _____

Name of piece _____
Meanings _____
_____

Name of piece _____
Meanings _____
_____

Name of piece _____
Meanings _____
_____

Name of piece _____
Meanings _____
_____

Name of piece _____
Meanings _____
_____

Name of piece _____
Meanings _____
_____

Name of piece _____
Meanings _____
_____

Name of piece _____
Meanings _____
_____

Name of piece _____
Meanings _____
_____

Name of piece _____
Meanings _____
_____

Name of piece _____
Meanings _____
_____

Name of piece _____
Meanings _____
_____

Name of piece _____
Meanings _____

Name of piece _____
Meanings _____
_____

Name of piece _____
Meanings _____
_____

Name of piece _____
Meanings _____
_____

Name of piece _____
Meanings _____
_____

Name of piece _____
Meanings _____
_____

Name of piece _____
Meanings _____

Name of piece _____
Meanings _____
_____

Name of piece _____
Meanings _____
_____

Name of piece _____
Meanings _____
_____

Name of piece _____
Meanings _____
_____

Name of piece _____
Meanings _____
_____

Name of piece _____
Meanings _____
_____

Name of piece _____
Meanings _____
_____

Name of piece _____
Meanings _____
_____

Name of piece _____
Meanings _____
_____

Name of piece _____
Meanings _____
_____

Name of piece _____
Meanings _____
_____

Name of piece _____
Meanings _____
_____

Name of piece _____
Meanings _____
_____

Name of piece _____
Meanings _____
_____

Name of piece _____
Meanings _____
_____

Name of piece _____
Meanings _____
_____

Name of piece _____
Meanings _____
_____

Name of piece _____
Meanings _____
_____

Name of piece _____
Meanings _____

Name of piece _____
Meanings _____
_____

Name of piece _____
Meanings _____
_____

Name of piece _____
Meanings _____
_____

Name of piece _____
Meanings _____
_____

Name of piece _____
Meanings _____
_____

Name of piece _____
Meanings _____
_____

Name of piece _____
Meanings _____
_____

Name of piece _____
Meanings _____
_____

Name of piece _____
Meanings _____
_____

Name of piece _____
Meanings _____
_____

Name of piece _____
Meanings _____
_____

Name of piece _____
Meanings _____
_____

Name of piece _____
Meanings _____
_____

Name of piece _____
Meanings _____
_____

Tools used by other family members

This section is not exclusively for people who have known diviners in their family. Divination isn't always called what you think it is. Some families fiercely shun tarot cards but will readily tell you the meaning of a cloud formation as a sign of good luck to soon visit. Folded into different religious orders, divination may be referred the gift of prophecy. Noticing how your family has sought and received messages from God will be important for your practice, whether you continue in those ways or not. What are some ways others in your family divines? Write any other known methods of receiving messages in your family.

Family member/Ancestor _____
Method of divining _____
_____
Notes on method _____
_____
_____

Family member/Ancestor _____
Method of divining _____
_____
Notes on method _____
_____
_____

Family member/Ancestor _____
Method of divining _____
_____
Notes on method _____
_____
_____

Family member/Ancestor _____
Method of divining _____
_____
Notes on method _____
_____
_____

Family member/Ancestor _____
Method of divining _____

_____

Notes on method _____

_____

_____

Family member/Ancestor _____
Method of divining _____

_____

Notes on method _____

_____

_____

Family member/Ancestor _____
Method of divining _____

_____

Notes on method _____

_____

_____

Family member/Ancestor _____
Method of divining _____

_____

Notes on method _____

_____

_____

Family member/Ancestor _____
Method of divining _____

_____

Notes on method _____

_____

_____

12 SYMBOLISM

The way we culturally see the world is unique, and important to decoding our spiritual mysteries. Across magical systems, certain items carry specific meanings. There may be a universal meaning of a certain tree, yet a very specific one personal to you. Some folks may see a deer as a symbol of innocence and grace, but to some, it could be confirmation of a certain lineage of ancestors letting you know they're nearby. While it's useful to know both, for this book, try to use these spaces below to write symbolism that is personal and ancestral, rather than notations pulled from reference books. Defining the specific personal meaning of a thing will serve you best in divination and dream recall. If you're ever when you know you're receiving a message and you're stuck on deciphering, close your eyes, and ask, "What does this mean to me? And how can I best make sense of it?" Wait for a response and note what comes to you. Note and know that in the tradition of Hoodoo, it isn't uncommon for spirits to take the form of animals, plants, weather, or other things they favor whether in dreams or even in waking life...

In the sections ahead, note symbolism of various things for the purpose of deciphering messages. Save any ritualistic meanings and significances for later sections.

Animal Symbolism

The screeching of an owl at midnight, the flight of a crow through a crossroads, and even the sign of a red cardinal invoke reactions to each of us. Animals can convey various messages in both overt and subtle ways. Along with any warnings or beautiful confirmations, they remind us to step outside of the scope of our daily lives to seek Spirit in some of the most natural ways. Use this section to note messages you've come across about the symbolic meanings of various animals, or information shared with you from ancestors, elders, and community members.

Animal _____

Meanings/Representation _____

_____

_____

Spirits connected or sacred to it _____

_____

_____

Notes/knowing's found about this animal _____

_____

_____

_____

Animal _____

Meanings/Representation _____

_____

_____

Spirits connected or sacred to it _____

_____

_____

Notes/knowing's found about this animal _____

_____

_____

_____

Animal _____

Meanings/Representation _____

_____

_____

Spirits connected or sacred to it _____
_____
_____

Notes/knowing's found about this animal _____
_____
_____

Animal _____
Meanings/Representation _____
_____
_____

Spirits connected or sacred to it _____
_____
_____

Notes/knowing's found about this animal _____
_____
_____

Animal _____
Meanings/Representation _____
_____
_____

Spirits connected or sacred to it _____
_____
_____

Notes/knowing's found about this animal _____
_____
_____

Plant Symbolism

Just as much as messages from the animal kingdom can remind us to seek spirit in nature, messages from the plant world can slow us down to listen. Dreaming of the pine trees that lined your family's driveway has a specific message, that could have been ancestral sent to you. Seeing various morning glories, hearing them frequently brought up in conversation, and randomly smelling them could convey a special message from a spirit that the plant is sacred to. Use this section to note messages you've come across about the symbolic meanings of various plants, or information shared with you from ancestors, elders, and community members.

Plant _____

Meanings/Representation _____

_____

_____

Spirits connected or sacred to it _____

_____

_____

Notes/knowings found about this plant _____

_____

_____

_____

Plant _____

Meanings/Representation _____

_____

_____

Spirits connected or sacred to it _____

_____

_____

Notes/knowings found about this plant _____

_____

_____

Plant _____

Meanings/Representation _____

_____

_____

Spirits connected or sacred to it _____
_____
_____

Notes/knowing's found about this plant _____
_____
_____

Plant _____
Meanings/Representation _____
_____

Spirits connected or sacred to it _____
_____
_____

Notes/knowing's found about this plant _____
_____
_____

Plant _____
Meanings/Representation _____
_____

Spirits connected or sacred to it _____
_____
_____

Notes/knowing's found about this plant _____
_____
_____

Weather

Weather phenomena are often how the Creator and its various spiritual children will communicate with us at one time. Once you go past the common symbolic meanings of each phenomenon, you allow yourself to hear the significance and sometimes hidden language of each phenomenon. A large hurricane approaching a town could spell great tragedy for many. But for a few, they'll hear the whispers of how this storm may hold the breakthrough they've been praying for. Be especially aware of how these phenomena color our dreams, as they can take entirely new connotations in the astral realm.

In the spaces ahead, note findings and knowings when it comes to symbolism around various weather phenomena

Clouds

Meanings/representations _____
_____
_____

Spirits connected or sacred to it _____
_____
_____

Messages received from specific phenomena _____
_____
_____

Rain

Meanings/representations _____
_____
_____

Spirits connected or sacred to it _____
_____
_____

Messages received from specific phenomena _____
_____
_____

Floods

Meanings/representations _____
_____
_____

Spirits connected or sacred to it _____
_____
_____

Messages received from specific phenomena _____
_____
_____

Fog

Meanings/representations _____
_____
_____

Spirits connected or sacred to it _____
_____
_____

Messages received from specific phenomena _____
_____
_____

Wind

Meanings/representations _____
_____
_____

Spirits connected or sacred to it _____
_____
_____

Messages received from specific phenomena _____
_____
_____

Thunderstorms

Meanings/representations _____
_____
_____

Spirits connected or sacred to it _____
_____
_____

Messages received from specific phenomena _____
_____
_____

Hailstorm

Meanings/representations _____
_____
_____

Spirits connected or sacred to it _____
_____
_____

Messages received from specific phenomena _____
_____
_____

Hurricanes

Meanings/representations _____
_____
_____

Spirits connected or sacred to it _____
_____
_____

Messages received from specific phenomena _____
_____
_____

Lightning

Meanings/representations _____
_____
_____

Spirits connected or sacred to it _____
_____
_____

Messages received from specific phenomena _____
_____
_____

Tornado

Meanings/representations _____
_____
_____

Spirits connected or sacred to it _____
_____
_____

Messages received from specific phenomena _____
_____
_____

Flood

Meanings/representations _____
_____
_____

Spirits connected or sacred to it _____
_____
_____

Messages received from specific phenomena _____
_____
_____

Snow

Meanings/representations _____
_____
_____

Spirits connected or sacred to it _____
_____
_____

Messages received from specific phenomena _____
_____
_____

Frost

Meanings/representations _____
_____
_____

Spirits connected or sacred to it _____
_____
_____

Messages received from specific phenomena _____
_____
_____

Earthquake

Meanings/representations _____
_____
_____

Spirits connected or sacred to it _____
_____
_____

Messages received from specific phenomena _____
_____
_____

Numbers

Number symbolism plays a huge role in Hoodoo. Some rituals are consecutive, continuing for a set number of days. Certain times of day and night are more desirable to conjure for certain things, as opposed to others. Some of these numerological references practitioners observe trace to African Traditional Religions, Christianity, Hebrew Mysticism, and other systems. However, as stated in previous sections, personal and ancestral connections to numbers will serve you best. When numbers are highlighted throughout your day, your personal and ancestral implication of the number will surpass any universal definition.

Along each number, write your personal notes and learnings about its energy. Purposefully not included are repetitions or angel numbers, as in their simplistic definition, they're amplified messages of the original meaning of the number.

1 _____
_____
_____

2 _____
_____
_____

3 _____
_____
_____

4 _____
_____
_____

5 _____
_____
_____

6 _____
_____
_____

7 _____

_____

_____

8 _____

_____

_____

9 _____

_____

_____

10 _____

_____

_____

11 _____

_____

_____

13 _____

_____

_____

Prime numbers _____

_____

_____

Even numbers _____

_____

_____

Odd numbers _____

_____

_____

Objects of significance

Many mundane items have great significance in Hoodoo. This is where cultural and ancestral context can come into play. A broom may have the symbolic significance of cleansing, but maybe your Auntie used them while chasing you and your cousins when y'all would sass mouth. In that case, when you see a broom in your dreams or waking life, it could be a warning to watch that mouth. You can include anecdotal meanings of items from stories, songs, and poems. However, I would be mindful of garnering meanings about objects from TV and film. Many African traditional and derived religions are sensationalized on TV and film. The meaning and significance of objects will often get distorted for entertainment. Every region, every family, and every practitioner have different understandings and uses of objects.

Object _____
Meaning/Representation _____
_____
_____
_____

Spirits connected or sacred to it _____
_____
_____

Additional notes/knowings found about this object _____
_____
_____
_____

Object _____
Meaning/Representation _____
_____
_____
_____

Spirits connected or sacred to it _____
_____
_____

Additional notes/knowings found about this object _____
_____

_____

_____

Object _____
Meaning/Representation _____

_____

_____

_____

Spirits connected or sacred to it _____

_____

_____

Additional notes/knowings found about this object _____

_____

_____

_____

Object _____
Meaning/Representation _____

_____

_____

_____

Spirits connected or sacred to it _____

_____

_____

Additional notes/knowings found about this object _____

_____

_____

_____

Buildings

Every building has its own spiritual significance. A dreamed-up conversation about your friend's cheating boyfriend happening in a beauty shop has a specific weight to it, versus if it were to take place in a courtroom, or even your childhood bedroom. Any of these scenarios could happen, but the room where it happens must be considered when deciphering messages. The environment is almost as important as what happens. Certain spirits may not show themselves in a dream or a vision, but their domain could subtly alert you of their presence. Or your spirit guides delivering a message may make use of a building you're familiar with to connect memories and themes to layer a message.

Type of building _____
Meaning/Representation _____
_____
_____
Spirits connected or sacred to it _____
_____
_____
Additional notes/knowings about this building _____
_____
_____
_____

Type of building _____
Meaning/Representation _____
_____
_____
Spirits connected or sacred to it _____
_____
Additional notes/knowings about this building _____
_____
_____
_____

Type of building _____

Meaning/Representation _____

_____

_____

Spirits connected or sacred to it _____

_____

_____

Additional notes/knowings about this building _____

_____

_____

_____

Type of building _____

Meaning/Representation _____

_____

_____

Spirits connected or sacred to it _____

_____

_____

Additional notes/knowings about this building _____

_____

_____

_____

Type of building _____

Meaning/Representation _____

_____

_____

Spirits connected or sacred to it _____

_____

_____

Additional notes/knowings about this building _____

_____

_____

_____

Landscapes/Places

Close your eyes when you walk by a crossroads. Just for a moment. Even in silence, you'll feel energy emanating from this transient nexus. Do the same at a river, in the woods, or even at your local marketplace. Various impressions will flash before your mind's eye, and before you know it, you'll catch the definable meanings of each place. Some are obvious. While other meanings and definitions may need help garnered from ancestors, elders, and community members. Just as in the section before, be aware of the influence of spirits and spirit guides with landscapes. Even more than buildings, certain landscapes are sacred to certain spirits. In both waking and dreaming life, if you notice a sign being delivered in a certain landscape, be aware of this layer.

Name of place _____

Meaning/Representation _____

_____

Spirits connected or sacred to it _____

_____

Additional notes/knowings about this place _____

_____

_____

_____

Name of place _____

Meaning/Representation _____

_____

Spirits connected or sacred to it _____

_____

Additional notes/knowings about this place _____

_____

_____

_____

Name of place _____
Meaning/Representation _____
_____
_____

Spirits connected or sacred to it _____
_____
_____

Additional notes/knowings about this place _____
_____
_____
_____

Name of place _____
Meaning/Representation _____
_____
_____

Spirits connected or sacred to it _____
_____
_____

Additional notes/knowings about this place _____
_____
_____
_____

Name of place _____
Meaning/Representation _____
_____
_____

Spirits connected or sacred to it _____
_____

Additional notes/knowings about this place _____
_____
_____
_____

13 DREAMS

From the moment you close those heavy eyes to the moment they struggle to open lies a world of events. Heavily layered instructions can be bestowed to a dreamer within a matter of seconds. Ancestors can visit to deliver warnings. Higher spirits can perform entire rituals. And you could see your high school crush deliver you a milkshake from a drive-through window wearing a cowboy costume, all within one night. Many people brush off most of their dreams until they feel one or two to be truly urgent. It is true that within the first few moments of waking, dreams often fade from our memory as we become more lucid. It's of high importance to pay attention to our dreams as Hoodoos. This is where the symbolism of the previous chapter will come to play. Our spiritual court will often play upon our own understandings of the world to deliver nuanced messages we need to decipher. We can seek council, but sometimes it will be up to the dreamer to unlock the meaning for themselves. If you don't dream much, or at all, don't fear. While some folks are naturally more vivid dreamers, it can be nurtured. Pay attention to how you prepare yourself for sleep and the care you take to get into bed. Be mindful of the substances you consume before bed. Try turning off distractions a few hours ahead of sleep, choose tea like mugwort or lavender, and set the intention with prayer or candle to receive messages from specific ancestors or spirit guides.

In the pages ahead, note your knowings & findings in this realm

Dream Recall

Use section ahead to begin your dream recall work. For 7 days, write as much as you can of your dreams when you first wake up. Don't focus so hard on interpretation when writing. Just jot down the things that happen, colors, symbols, sounds, settings, people that appear, and the things that they say. Sometimes, you'll instantly be able to decipher meanings. Other times, you'll only understand a dream after new information has been presented. Some people keep dream journals that last months, or years. Let this section start you out or allow you to return to it.

Date _____

Dream _____

_____

_____

_____

_____

_____

_____

_____

_____

_____

_____

Date _____

Dream _____

_____

_____

_____

_____

_____

_____

_____

_____

_____

_____

Date _____
Dream _____
_____
_____
_____
_____
_____
_____
_____
_____

Date _____
Dream _____
_____
_____
_____
_____
_____
_____
_____
_____
_____

Date _____
Dream _____
_____
_____
_____
_____
_____
_____
_____
_____

Date _____
Dream _____
_____
_____
_____
_____
_____
_____
_____
_____
_____

Date _____
Dream _____
_____
_____
_____
_____
_____
_____
_____
_____
_____

Sleep Rituals

The care taken when laying your body to rest is vital. Beyond just washing your face, greasing your scalp, and brushing your teeth, your mind, body, and spirit must wind down to be prepared for good rest. What rituals and prayers do you do to ensure good sleep? Do you have any protections you place in your room? Is there anything you use to enhance prophetic dreams? Any foods or teas you'll prepare for good sleep? Use the space below to jot down any sleep rituals you use, and their purpose.

14 ANCESTRAL ALTAR

Ancestral veneration is a vital pillar of Hoodoo. Setting your altar space will be an intimate (and individual) process between you and your ancestors. This is the point of convergence between the physical and ancestral realm. It is here where we both seek their counsel, and can deliver offerings for spirits in need of recognition and elevation. It can be an elaborate table, ordained with candles, pictures, plants, and food. Or it can be a family bible with a few letters and pictures tucked inside. There may be certain foundational elements that are common amongst practitioners, but yours shouldn't and won't look exactly like anyone else's. No one has your Uncle that used to tell the same stories about the good ole days, of chasin' women, and slicking his hair back with murray's pomade and his favorite brush. Nor does anyone have your Grandma that used her wooden spoon to both offer you some cornbread batter, and pop you or your siblings when you got outta line. These items, and the placement of them, will tell the story of your relationship with these ancestors, and how they can show up for you, spiritually.

In the pages ahead, note your knowings & findings in this realm

What are the foundational elements of your altar? What keys things must you use to call your ancestors into place? _____

_____

_____

_____

_____

_____

_____

_____

Where is your altar set? Indoors or outdoors? If indoors, what room? If outdoors, where at? _____

_____

How often do you tend to it? Certain day of the day/week/month? Certain times of day? _____

What are some favorite meals your ancestors request? Certain drinks? Candies? Fruits? *(This will and should change. Just as much as we don't always eat the menu from Thanksgiving on a weekly basis, use this space to jot down and keep track of what you 'hear' them say for you to fix for them.)* _____

_____

_____

_____

_____

_____

_____

_____

_____

_____

What personal items do you have for your ancestors? *Jot down the item, and the person it's for.* _____

_____

_____

_____

_____

_____

_____

What gifts or tools do you have for your ancestors? _____

_____

_____

_____

_____

What protections do you set on your altar? _____
_____
_____
_____
_____

What are some taboos you have about your altar? _____
_____
_____
_____
_____
_____

What are some workings or rituals you do specifically with your ancestral altar? _____
_____
_____
_____
_____
_____
_____
_____
_____
_____
_____
_____

What are some workings or rituals you do *for* your ancestors? *(Elevation, cleansing, healing, empowering, etc)* _____
_____
_____
_____
_____
_____
_____
_____
_____

15 CLEANSING SELF

We all learn different aspects of our craft in different parts of our path. For beginners, it is suggested to learning cleansing work first, as this is something that will sustain your entire spiritual walk and will be necessary for all other work. A good cleansing routine will mitigate spiritual attacks and most spiritual mistakes. Cleansing first requires the removal of negativity or attachments, followed by purification, and then blessing. Some rituals will encompass these steps in one swoop. Others will be more definitive. For this journal, we'll break down the steps to better define what can be used in which process. Some things will fit in more than one area. As comprehensive and complex as this chapter may be, cleansing can often be quite simple. Sometimes, just a drop of oil, a fierce song, or fervent hand clapping will cleanse the soul of a compounded curse. The ultimate underlying factor is faith.

In the pages ahead, note your knowings & findings in this realm

What things do you use to **remove** negative attachments, spirits, energy, curses, hexes?

Roots & Herbs _____

_____

_____

_____

Waters _____

_____

Dirts _____

_____

Incense _____

_____

Crystals _____

_____

Symbols _____

_____

Animals _____

_____

Songs _____

_____

Prayers _____

_____

Scriptures _____

_____

Poems _____

_____

Other _____

What things do you use for **purification** of mind, body, spirit?

Roots & Herbs _____

_____

_____

_____

Waters _____

_____

Dirts _____

_____

Incense _____

_____

Crystals _____

_____

Symbols _____

_____

Animals _____

_____

Songs _____

_____

Prayers _____

_____

Scriptures _____

_____

Poems _____

_____

Other _____

What things do you use for **blessing**, and the invitation of goodness into your life?

Roots & Herbs _____

_____

_____

_____

_____

Waters _____

_____

Dirts _____

_____

Incense _____

_____

Crystals _____

_____

Symbols _____

_____

Animals _____

_____

Songs _____

_____

Prayers _____

_____

Scriptures _____

_____

Poems _____

_____

Other _____

What are some early signs, warnings, or omens of incoming negativity, curses, hexes, or malevolent spirits? _____

_____

_____

_____

_____

_____

_____

What are some divination styles or spreads you use to determine if a cleansing is needed?

_____

_____

_____

_____

_____

_____

_____

_____

_____

_____

_____

What ancestors were known to cleanse others? *Conjurors, Rootworkers, Healers, Preachers, Priests, Pastors, etc.* _____

_____

_____

_____

_____

_____

_____

_____

_____

_____

Are there any spirit guides or entities you call on for cleansing? _____
_____
_____
_____
_____
_____
_____
_____
_____
_____
_____
_____
_____

What day or days of the week, month, and year do you associate with cleansing, breakthrough, and blessing? _____
_____
_____

What numbers do you associate with cleansing, breakthrough, and blessing? _____
_____
_____

What colors do you associate with cleansing, breakthrough, and blessing? _____
_____
_____

Write down the various times throughout the day, and the type of cleansing/breakthroughs that could occur (mornings, twilight, midnight, etc)

Before dawn _____
Morning _____
Afternoon _____
Evening _____
Dusk _____
Night _____
Midnight _____

Cleanings oil recipes? _____

_____

_____

_____

_____

_____

_____

_____

_____

Cleansing baths? _____

_____

_____

_____

_____

_____

_____

_____

_____

_____

_____

Cleansing powder recipes? _____

_____

_____

_____

_____

_____

_____

_____

_____

_____

Cleansing candle formulas? _____
_____
_____
_____
_____
_____
_____
_____
_____
_____

Other cleansing, breakthrough, and blessing rituals? _____
_____
_____
_____
_____
_____
_____
_____
_____
_____
_____
_____

Places to bury cleansing workings? _____
_____
_____
_____
_____
_____
_____
_____
_____
_____
_____

What are some successful cleansing workings you have performed?

_____

_____

_____

_____

_____

_____

_____

_____

_____

_____

_____

_____

_____

_____

_____

_____

_____

_____

_____

_____

_____

_____

_____

_____

_____

_____

_____

_____

_____

16 CLEANSING HOME

Whether you woke up to sounds of Anita Baker, Patti LaBelle, Luther Vandross or any gospel, funk, or jazz record beckoning you to get up and start cleaning on a Saturday morning, these vibrations told you what time it was. Smells of Ajax & pine sol would fill the air, and any dust bunny or boo hag knew it was time to run. Cleansing your home is as important as cleansing yourself. In its basic form, it's the manipulation of a microcosm to affect your macrocosm. Home cleansing work encapsulates physically cleaning, as well as ritualistic cleansing, banishing, blessing, and protecting a space. What you do in your home will affect your life at large. If your home is dirty and confusing, then your life will reflect. However, don't take this notion to an obsessive extreme. If you can't clean your home to your liking, please know that you are still worthy of blessings. It's about doing what you can when you can and asking for help when available. Home cleansing rituals are often the most common Hoodoo rituals still passed down through families.

In the pages ahead, note your knowings & findings in this realm

What are some signs, warnings, and omens the energy of your home is off and in need of a cleansing? _____

_____

_____

_____

_____

_____

What are some divination styles or spreads you use to discern how to cleanse your home? _____

_____

_____

_____

_____

_____

_____

_____

_____

_____

What are some preventative measures you take to ensure your home is spiritually safe?

_____

_____

_____

_____

_____

_____

_____

_____

_____

What are some workings or rituals you use to banish any unwanted energies from your home? _____

_____

_____

_____

_____

_____

_____

_____

What ancestors were known to manage and successfully keep a home? *Not just matriarchs & patriarchs, but family members that led organizations and groups, or were involved in home related businesses* _____

_____

_____

_____

_____

_____

_____

_____

_____

_____

_____

What spirits or entities do you call on for home cleansing work? _____

_____

_____

_____

_____

_____

_____

_____

_____

_____

_____

_____

_____

What day or days of the week, month, and year did your family usually clean the house?

_____

_____

What numbers do you associate with home cleansing work? *Include numerological values of your home* _____

_____

_____

What colors do you associate with home cleansing work? _____
_____
_____

What roots/herbs that are local to you do you use for home cleansing work? _____
_____
_____
_____
_____
_____
_____
_____
_____

What roots/herbs do you use in general for home cleansing work? _____
_____
_____
_____
_____
_____
_____
_____
_____
_____

What waters do you use for home cleansing work? _____
_____
_____

What incense do you use for home cleansing work? _____
_____
_____

What crystals do you use for home cleansing work? _____
_____
_____

What symbols do you use for home cleansing work? _____
_____
_____

What are some animals you use for home cleansing work? _____
_____
_____

What are some tools you use for home cleansing work? _____
_____
_____

What songs do you use for home cleansing? _____
_____
_____
_____
_____
_____
_____
_____
_____

What prayers, scriptures, and poems do you use for home cleansing work? _____
_____
_____
_____
_____
_____
_____
_____

What are some rituals or movements done to cleanse the home (*clapping hands, sweeping from the back of the house to front, singing, etc*) _____
_____
_____
_____
_____
_____
_____
_____

What rituals do you do to invite blessings to an existing home? A new home? _____
_____
_____
_____
_____
_____
_____
_____

What are some workings or rituals you do to find a new home? _____
_____
_____
_____
_____
_____
_____
_____

Anointing oil recipes? _____
_____
_____
_____
_____
_____

Floorwash recipes? _____
_____
_____
_____
_____
_____
_____

Powder recipes? _____
_____
_____
_____
_____
_____
_____

Home blessing candle formuals? _____
_____
_____
_____
_____
_____
_____

Other home cleansing workings _____
_____
_____
_____
_____
_____
_____

Places to bury home cleansing work _____

_____

_____

_____

_____

_____

What are some successful home blessing workings you have performed? _____

_____

_____

_____

_____

_____

_____

_____

_____

_____

_____

_____

_____

_____

_____

_____

_____

_____

_____

_____

_____

_____

_____

_____

_____

17 HEALING

Healing is not just an individual responsibility. If one person in the community is unwell, it affects the entire community, whether or not the illness is contagious. It is crucial in Hoodoo that we perceive healing beyond just ourselves, but towards an investment in our community's wellbeing. It is said that each illness is its own spirit. So, removing illness can often be like removing an entity or attachment. There must be a dissolve of any agreements between the host and illness, then cleansing and strengthening to bring the ill one back to health. In some cases, an illness must be trapped in a container such as a bottle, an egg, a symbol, an animal, etc. Use the prompts below to journal your healing correspondences and knowings.

Note: This is section is primarily for the spiritual process of healing. This is not intended to document medicinal properties, whether holistic or western. Spiritual healing can use any physical means to gain the intended goal of health. Be mindful of this when engaging in healing magic.

In the pages ahead, note your knowings & findings in this realm

What are some early spiritual signs and warnings to alarm you of potential illness? ___

_____
_____
_____
_____
_____
_____
_____

What are some divination styles or spreads you use to determine an overview of health?

_____

_____

_____

_____

_____

_____

_____

_____

_____

_____

What preventative measures do you take to spiritually ward off illness? _____

_____

_____

_____

_____

_____

_____

_____

_____

_____

_____

What ways do you spiritually cleanse the body of illness? _____

_____

_____

_____

_____

_____

_____

_____

_____

_____

_____

What ancestors were known healers? *Conjurors, Rootworkers, Midwives, Nurses, Doctors, etc.*

_____

_____

_____

_____

_____

_____

_____

_____

_____

Are there any spirit guides or entities you call on for help/intercession in healing? ____

_____

_____

_____

_____

_____

_____

_____

_____

_____

_____

_____

What day or days of the week, month, and year do you associate with healing? _____

_____

_____

What numbers do you associate with healing? _____

_____

_____

What colors do you associate with healing? _____

_____

_____

What roots/herbs naturally grow around you that foster healing? _____
_____
_____
_____
_____
_____
_____
_____
_____

What roots/herbs in general do you use for healing? _____
_____
_____
_____
_____
_____
_____
_____

What are some healing waters you use? _____
_____

What are some healing dirts you use? _____
_____

What are some healing incenses you use? _____
_____

What are some healing crystals you use? _____
_____
_____

What are some healing symbols you use? _____
_____
_____

What are some animals you use in healing work? _____
_____
_____

What other spiritual tools do you use for healing work? _____
_____
_____

Songs of healing? _____
_____
_____
_____
_____
_____
_____
_____
_____
_____

Prayers, scriptures, poems of healing? _____
_____
_____
_____
_____
_____
_____
_____

What are some workings & rituals you use to call for strength and vitality after sickness?

_____
_____
_____
_____
_____
_____
_____
_____

What are some workings & rituals you do to maintain good health?

_____
_____
_____
_____
_____
_____
_____
_____

What are some workings & rituals you do ward off sickness from entry into your life?

_____
_____
_____
_____
_____
_____
_____
_____

Healing oil recipes? _____

_____
_____
_____
_____
_____
_____

Healing bath recipes? _____
_____
_____
_____
_____
_____
_____

Healing powder recipes? _____
_____
_____
_____
_____
_____
_____

Healing candle formulas? _____
_____
_____
_____
_____
_____
_____

Other healing rituals? _____
_____
_____
_____
_____
_____
_____

Places to bury healing workings _____

_____

_____

_____

_____

_____

What are some successful healing workings you have performed?

_____

_____

_____

_____

_____

_____

_____

_____

_____

_____

_____

_____

_____

_____

_____

_____

_____

_____

_____

_____

_____

18 PROTECTION

Cleansing and healing work means nothing if we don't fortify and arm ourselves with protection. For some people, protection magic is the only magic they know how to perform. The public may not believe in benevolent magic, but most folks know just enough to avoid baneful magic. Ask someone for a loc of their hair and see how their face turns up. Good protection can block dangerous things from happening in your life that would lead you astray. Active protection can snuff out shady friends, harmful spirits, and even opportunities that would ultimately sour. If you are engaged in spiritual warfare, or an overzealous enemy, you will need varying types of protection. Keeping track of your protection work is important, as is being flexible to adjust it depending on what circumstances come your way.

In the pages ahead, note your knowings & findings in this realm

What are some early signs, warnings, and omens of protection work being necessary or current work fading? _____

_____

_____

_____

_____

_____

_____

What are some divinations styles or spreads you use to determine if protection work is needed or has faded? _____

_____
_____
_____
_____
_____
_____
_____
_____

What are some ways you maintain and feed existing protection work? _____

_____
_____
_____
_____
_____
_____
_____
_____
_____
_____

What ancestors do you consider the protectors of the family, and in what ways? _____

_____
_____
_____
_____
_____
_____
_____
_____
_____

Are there any spirit guides or entities you call on for power and protection? _____

_____

_____

_____

_____

_____

_____

_____

_____

_____

What days of the week, month, and year do you associate with protection? _____

_____

_____

What numbers do you associate with protections? _____

_____

_____

What colors do you associate with protection? _____

_____

_____

What roots/herbs naturally grow around you that you consider protective? _____

_____

_____

_____

_____

_____

_____

_____

_____

_____

_____

What roots/herbs in general do you use for protection? _____
_____
_____
_____
_____
_____
_____
_____
_____
_____
_____
_____
_____
_____

What are some protective waters you use? _____
_____
_____

What are protective dirts you use? _____
_____
_____

What are some protective incenses you use? _____
_____
_____

What are some protective crystals you use? _____
_____
_____

What are some protective symbols you use? _____
_____
_____

What are some animals you use in protection work? _____
_____
_____

What are some tools you use in protection work? _____
_____
_____

What are some songs you use in protection work? _____
_____
_____
_____
_____
_____
_____
_____
_____

Prayers, scriptures, poems of protection? _____
_____
_____
_____
_____
_____
_____
_____
_____
_____

What are some workings & rituals you do to call for protection?
_____
_____
_____
_____
_____
_____
_____
_____

Protection oil recipes? _____
_____
_____
_____
_____
_____
_____
_____
_____

Protection bath recipes? _____
_____
_____
_____
_____
_____
_____
_____

Protection powder recipes? _____
_____
_____
_____
_____
_____
_____
_____

Protection candle formulas? _____
_____
_____
_____
_____
_____
_____
_____

Places to bury protection workings _____
_____
_____
_____
_____
_____

What are some successful protection workings you have performed?

_____
_____
_____
_____
_____
_____
_____
_____
_____
_____
_____
_____
_____
_____
_____
_____
_____
_____
_____
_____
_____
_____
_____
_____

19 PROSPERITY

One of the most popular and sought-after types of workings is prosperity and money. Over time, you'll notice with this type of conjure that if you're not addressing the underlying issues of your finances, the work won't be as effective. Many have great luck conjuring money in the beginning of their magical studies, but over time may loop back into the same situations. The lessons that come with money workings are ones of self-worth, personal power, boundaries, time management, and more.

It's worth noting there are systemic issues at play that affect our relationships with money. Behind those systemic issues are the spiritual influences this country was built upon. However, that doesn't mean you, as a Hoodoo descendant, are destined to be in lack. The overall goal of money workings is to erase the fear of personal power, abundance, and, of course, bring more money and ease into our lives.

Added into this section are mentions of road opening workings. Road openers are a traditional working in Hoodoo to remove obstacles prohibiting you from your goals and intended desires. While road openers can be use towards love goals, health goals, and any intended road one can name, the prompts are added within this section to further help users in their prosperity goals.

In the pages ahead, note your knowings & findings in this realm

What are some early spiritual signs, warnings, or omens to alarm you of money jinxes, curses, & blockages around finance? *(focus on things other than just low funds. An omen could come in the form of a nightmare of a shady business partner, an itching of the wrong palm, etc.)* _____

_____

_____

_____

_____

_____

_____

_____

What are some divination styles or spreads you use to see an overview of money situations? _____

_____

_____

_____

_____

_____

_____

_____

_____

What preventative measures do you take to spiritually protect your money, business, job, & success in general? _____

_____

_____

_____

_____

_____

_____

_____

What are some superstitions and taboos you avoid around money, business, jobs, & success in general? _____

_____

_____

_____

_____

_____

_____

_____

What are some spiritual signs you recognize about money and luck coming in? _____

_____

_____

_____

_____

_____

_____

_____

_____

_____

_____

What ancestors were known to lucky in life and or great with money? *Worked in commission sales? Gamblers? Numbers runners?*_____

_____

_____

_____

_____

_____

_____

_____

_____

What ancestors were business owners and or great with money management? *Farmers?*
Accountants? _____

_____

_____

_____

_____

_____

_____

_____

_____

Are there any spirit guides or entities you call on for money work? Opening roads? Fast
luck? Success? Business matters? _____

_____

_____

_____

_____

_____

_____

_____

_____

What days of the week, month, and year do you associate with money? Opening roads?
Fast luck? Success? Business matters? _____

_____

_____

_____

_____

_____

_____

_____

What numbers do you associate with money? Opening roads? Fast luck? Success? Business matters? _____

_____

_____

_____

_____

_____

_____

_____

_____

What colors do you associate with money? Opening roads? Fast luck? Success? Business matters? _____

_____

_____

_____

_____

_____

_____

_____

_____

_____

_____

What roots/herbs naturally grow around you that bring money? Opening roads? Fast luck? Success? Business matters? _____

_____

_____

_____

_____

_____

_____

_____

_____

What roots/herbs in general do you use for money work? Opening roads? Fast luck? Success? Business matters? _____

_____

_____

_____

_____

_____

_____

_____

_____

_____

What are some waters you use in your money work? Opening roads? Fast luck? Success? Business matters? _____

_____

_____

_____

_____

_____

_____

_____

_____

_____

What are some dirts you use for your money work? Opening roads? Fast luck? Success? Business matters? _____

_____

_____

_____

_____

_____

_____

_____

_____

What are some incenses you for money work? Opening roads? Fast luck? Success? Business matters? _____

_____

_____

_____

_____

_____

_____

_____

_____

_____

What are some crystals you use for money work? Opening roads? Fast luck? Success? Business matters? _____

_____

_____

_____

_____

_____

_____

_____

_____

_____

What are some symbols you use for money work? Opening roads? Fast luck? Success? Business matters? _____

_____

_____

_____

_____

_____

_____

_____

_____

_____

What animals do you use in your money work? Opening roads? Fast luck? Success? Business matters? _____

_____

_____

_____

_____

_____

_____

_____

_____

_____

What are some tools you use for money work? Opening roads? Fast luck? Success? Business matters? _____

_____

_____

_____

_____

_____

_____

_____

_____

_____

Songs about money? Opening roads? Fast luck? Success? Business matters? _____

_____

_____

_____

_____

_____

_____

_____

_____

_____

Prayers, scriptures, poems about money? Opening roads? Fast luck? Success? Business matters? _____

_____

_____

_____

_____

_____

_____

_____

_____

What are some workings & rituals you use to banish money obstacles? _____

_____

_____

_____

_____

_____

_____

_____

_____

_____

_____

_____

What are some workings & rituals you use to open your roads? _____

_____

_____

_____

_____

_____

_____

_____

_____

_____

_____

What are some workings & rituals you use to bring in money? _____

_____

_____

_____

_____

_____

_____

_____

_____

_____

_____

What are some rituals you use to sustain finances? _____

_____

_____

_____

_____

_____

_____

_____

_____

_____

_____

What are some workings & rituals to bring success towards ventures? _____

_____

_____

_____

_____

_____

_____

_____

_____

_____

What are some workings & rituals to bring business and career success? _____
_____
_____
_____
_____
_____
_____
_____
_____
_____

What are some workings & rituals you do protect your money? _____
_____
_____
_____
_____
_____
_____
_____
_____
_____
_____
_____

Money oil recipes? Road Opener oil recipes? Fast luck oil recipes? Success oil recipes?
Better business oil recipes? _____
_____
_____
_____
_____
_____
_____
_____
_____

Money bath recipes? Road Opener bath recipes? Fast luck bath recipes? Success bath recipes? Better business bath recipes? _____

_____

_____

_____

_____

_____

_____

_____

Money powder recipes? Road Opener powder recipes? Fast luck powder recipes? Success powder recipes? Better business powder recipes? _____

_____

_____

_____

_____

_____

_____

_____

Money candle formulas? Road Opener candle formulas? Fast luck candle formulas? Success candle formulas? Better business candle formulas? _____

_____

_____

_____

_____

_____

_____

_____

Places to bury money work? Road openers? Fast luck? Success? Business matters? ____
_____
_____
_____
_____
_____
_____
_____
_____

What are some successful money, road opening, fast luck, success, or business workings you have performed? _____
_____
_____
_____
_____
_____
_____
_____
_____
_____
_____
_____
_____
_____
_____
_____
_____

20 LOVE

Right after money, the most sought-after type of conjure working is love magic. If you listen to old songs, stories, and books about conjure, our Hoodoo elders used love roots with many intentions. Whether to keep a family together during slavery, or to ensure an insecure lovers' need to control their partner; ethics and morals seem to vary case to case. Regardless of how controversial it may be, love magic is a cornerstone in conjure. You should lean on your inner moral compass, but more importantly, you should divine before initiating love work. Emotions can be funny, and while you may think a work was wildly unsuccessful, under the surface a raging fire could soon erupt in ways you never imagined.

Included in this section are prompts about emotional healing and self-love. In some families, this inner work is what may disrupt a familial curse that rolls down the line. A good self-love bath may even change your mind on lighting that 'come to me' candle.

In the pages ahead, note your knowings & findings in this realm

What spiritual signs, warnings, or omens have you noticed when a lover is a bad fit, or a relationship will soon be in turmoil? _____

_____

_____

_____

_____

_____

_____

_____

What are some divination styles or spreads you use to see and overview of a love situation? _____
_____
_____
_____
_____
_____
_____
_____
_____
_____
_____

What are some superstitions and taboos you avoid when dating someone? _____
_____
_____
_____
_____
_____
_____
_____
_____
_____
_____
_____

What ancestors were great with love, romance, and had great relationships? _____
_____
_____
_____
_____
_____
_____
_____
_____

Are there any spirit guides or entities you call on for love work? Attraction? Lust? Marriage? _____
_____
_____
_____
_____
_____
_____
_____
_____
_____
_____
_____

What day or days of the week, month, and year do you associate with love work? Attraction? Lust? Marriage? _____
_____
_____
_____
_____

What numbers do you associate with love work? Attraction? Lust? Marriage? _____
_____
_____
_____
_____

What colors do you associate with love work? Attraction? Lust? Marriage? _____
_____
_____
_____
_____

What roots/herbs naturally grow around you that bring love? Attraction? Lust? Marriage? _____
_____
_____
_____

_____
_____
_____
_____
_____
_____
_____
_____

What roots/herbs in general do you to use for love work? Attraction? Lust? Marriage?
_____
_____
_____
_____
_____
_____
_____
_____
_____
_____

What are some waters you use in your love work? Attraction? Lust? Marriage? _____
_____
_____
_____

What are some dirts you use in your love work? Attraction? Lust? Marriage? _____
_____
_____
_____

What are some incenses you use in your love work? Attraction? Lust? Marriage? _____
_____
_____
_____

What are some crystals you use in love work? Attraction? Lust? Marriage? _____

_____

_____

_____

_____

What are some symbols you use in love work? Attraction? Lust? Marriage? _____

_____

_____

_____

_____

What are some animals you use in your love work? Attraction? Lust? Marriage? _____

_____

_____

_____

_____

What are some tools you use in your love work? Attraction? Lust? Marriage? _____

_____

_____

_____

_____

Songs about love? Attraction? Lust? Marriage? _____

_____

_____

_____

_____

_____

_____

_____

_____

_____

_____

Prayers, scriptures, poems of love? Attraction? Lust? Marriage? _____

_____

_____

_____

_____

_____

_____

_____

_____

_____

What are some workings & rituals you use to cultivate self-love and draw your energy back to you? _____

_____

_____

_____

_____

_____

_____

_____

_____

_____

What are some workings & rituals you do to heal after breakups? _____

_____

_____

_____

_____

_____

_____

_____

_____

_____

_____

What are some workings & rituals you do to invite new love? _____
_____
_____
_____
_____
_____
_____
_____
_____
_____

What are some workings & rituals you do to remove blockages to love? _____
_____
_____
_____
_____
_____
_____
_____
_____
_____
_____

What are some workings & rituals you do to incite lust in another? _____
_____
_____
_____
_____
_____
_____
_____
_____
_____
_____

What are some workings & rituals you do to achieve a desired relationship title? _____
_____
_____
_____
_____
_____
_____
_____
_____
_____
_____
_____

What are some workings & rituals you do to sustain love in a relationship? _____
_____
_____
_____
_____
_____
_____
_____
_____
_____
_____
_____
_____

What are some workings and rituals you do protect your love? _____
_____
_____
_____
_____
_____
_____
_____
_____
_____
_____

Love oil recipes? Attraction oil recipes? Lust & sex oil recipes? Compelling & Influence oil recipes? Marriage oil recipes? _____

_____

_____

_____

_____

_____

_____

_____

_____

_____

Love bath recipes? Attraction bath recipes? Lust & sex bath recipes? Compelling & Influence bath recipes? Marriage bath recipes? _____

_____

_____

_____

_____

_____

_____

_____

_____

_____

Love powder recipes? Attraction powder recipes? Lust & sex powder recipes? Compelling & Influence powder recipes? Marriage powder recipes? _____

_____

_____

_____

_____

_____

_____

_____

_____

Love candle formulas? Attraction candle formulas? Lust & sex candle formulas? Compelling & Influence candle formulas? Marriage candle formulas?_____

_____

_____

_____

_____

_____

_____

_____

_____

Places to bury love workings? Attraction workings? Lust & sex workings? Compelling & Influence workings? Marriage workings? _____

_____

_____

_____

_____

_____

_____

_____

_____

What are some successful love workings you have performed? _____

_____

_____

_____

_____

_____

_____

_____

_____

_____

_____

_____

_____

_____

_____

_____

_____

_____

_____

_____

_____

_____

_____

_____

_____

_____

_____

_____

_____

_____

_____

_____

_____

_____

21 HEXES

Try as you might, left-handed work is necessary to learn for every practitioner. In Hoodoo, we don't believe in karma, but we believe in justice. Just as nature creates, it destroys to maintain balance. And as we are children of God, we must use our right hands and our left hands to maintain that balance. There are curses listed in almost every sacred and holy text. The key is timing and justification. This can be shown in divinations or signs. Just be mindful that even though you may have justification to lay a root on an enemy, you still need to take the proper precautions when doing this work.

Hexes and curses can be easily done with the right emotional charge but laying protections and following through with cleansing is what can separate a skilled practitioner from a novice ready to learn a potentially painful lesson.

In the pages ahead, note your knowings & findings in this realm

What are some divination styles or spreads you use to determine if a hex is justified? __

_____

_____

_____

_____

_____

_____

_____

Outside of divination, are there any signs of justification you look for when seeking confirmation of a hex? _____

_____

_____

_____

_____

_____

_____

_____

_____

_____

What ancestors were known to "take no mess", or actually practiced left handed work?

_____

_____

_____

_____

_____

_____

_____

_____

_____

Are there any spirit guides or entities you call on to assist with hexes? _____

_____

_____

_____

_____

_____

_____

_____

_____

_____

What day or days of the week, month, and year do you associate with hexes? _____
_____
_____

What numbers do you associate with hexes? _____
_____
_____

What colors do you associate with hexes? _____
_____
_____

What roots/herbs naturally grow around you that can be used for hexing? _____
_____
_____
_____
_____
_____
_____
_____
_____
_____
_____

What roots/herbs in general do you favor to use for hexing? _____
_____
_____
_____
_____
_____
_____
_____
_____
_____

What are some waters you use in your hexes? _____
_____
_____

What are some dirts you use in your hexes? _____
_____
_____

What are some incenses you use in your hexes? _____
_____
_____

What are some crystals you use for hexes? _____
_____
_____

What are some symbols you use for hexes? _____
_____
_____

What are some animals you use for hexes? _____
_____
_____

What are some tools you use for hexes? _____
_____
_____

Songs about hexes *(or aggression, rage, war, attacks)*? _____
_____
_____
_____
_____
_____
_____
_____

Prayers, scriptures, poems of retribution, curses, or hexes? _____
_____
_____
_____
_____
_____
_____
_____
_____
_____

What are some workings & rituals you use to remove or weaken a targets spiritual defense? _____
_____
_____
_____
_____
_____
_____
_____
_____
_____
_____

What are some workings & rituals you use to inflict harm on a target? _____
_____
_____
_____
_____
_____
_____
_____
_____
_____

What are some workings & rituals you use to influence or control a target? _____
_____
_____
_____
_____
_____
_____
_____
_____
_____
_____

What are some workings & rituals you use to keep a target down? _____
_____
_____
_____
_____
_____
_____
_____
_____
_____
_____
_____

What are some workings & rituals you do protect, hide, or cover yourself before or
during hex workings? _____
_____
_____
_____
_____
_____
_____
_____
_____

What ways do you cleanse yourself after performing a hex? _____

_____

_____

_____

_____

_____

_____

_____

Hex oil recipes? _____

_____

_____

_____

_____

_____

_____

_____

_____

_____

Hex potion recipes? _____

_____

_____

_____

_____

_____

_____

_____

_____

_____

Hex powder recipes? _____
_____
_____
_____
_____
_____
_____
_____
_____
_____
_____

Hexing candle formulas? _____
_____
_____
_____
_____
_____
_____
_____
_____
_____
_____
_____

Places to bury hex workings _____
_____
_____
_____
_____
_____
_____
_____
_____
_____
_____

What are some successful hexes you have performed? _____

_____

_____

_____

_____

_____

_____

_____

_____

_____

_____

_____

_____

_____

_____

_____

_____

_____

_____

_____

_____

_____

_____

_____

_____

_____

_____

_____

_____

_____

_____

_____

_____

_____

22 JUSTICE/COURT CASES

Of all the institutions in this country, the legal system is often the starkest reality of institutionalized racism. Because the odds are systematically stacked against us, it is in our best interest to call upon powers higher than ourselves when seeking justice. This could go from carrying High John while driving to avoid police, to petitioning and drawing up spirits to assist you in a legal payout. We don't have to fight these battles alone. Always be mindful of personal ethics and morals when considering justice and court case work. Of course, these vary from practitioner to practitioner. However, if you know you are in the "wrong", the weight of the work may come back to you in some form. If you are successful in getting off for a senseless murder, don't be surprised if you tragically lose a loved one. This is not karma. This is balance. And rectification works on its own timeline and can span generations. You could find yourself paying for the sins of an ancestor or picking up an unfinished fight for justice. This is all within the realm of court case work, and there are spirits, roots, and energies to help you gain victory.

In the pages ahead, note your knowings & findings in this realm

What are some spiritual signs, warnings, and omens you recognize regarding court cases, police, the legal system? _____

_____

_____

_____

_____

_____

_____

What are some superstitions and taboos you avoid for court case and legal situations?
_____
_____
_____
_____
_____
_____
_____
_____
_____
_____

What are some divination styles or spreads you use to see all facets and possibilities surrounding court case and legal work? _____
_____
_____
_____
_____
_____
_____
_____
_____
_____

What ancestors do you have that worked in the legal system? *Government? Or governed your family?* _____
_____
_____
_____
_____
_____
_____
_____

What ancestors do you have that were considered outlaws? *Either by trade, or successfully worked outside of law for some time of their lives.* _____

_____

_____

_____

_____

_____

_____

_____

_____

_____

Are there any spirit guides or entities you call on for help with court cases, police, the legal system? _____

_____

_____

_____

_____

_____

_____

_____

_____

_____

_____

_____

What day or days of the week, month, and year do you associate with law, order, and governing powers? _____

_____

_____

What numbers do you associate with law, order, and governing powers? _____

_____

_____

What colors do you associate with law, power, and government? _____

_____

_____

What roots/herbs naturally grow around you bring success in court case & legal workings? _____

_____

_____

_____

_____

_____

_____

_____

_____

_____

_____

_____

What roots/herbs in general do you like to use for court case & legal workings? _____

_____

_____

_____

_____

_____

_____

_____

_____

_____

_____

_____

_____

_____

What are some waters you use in court case and legal workings? _____

_____

_____

What are some dirts you use in court case and legal workings? _____

_____

_____

What are some incenses you use in court case and legal workings? _____

_____

_____

What are some crystals you use in court case and legal workings? _____
_____
_____

What are some animals you use in court case and legal workings? _____
_____
_____

What are some tools you use in court case and legal workings? _____
_____
_____

Songs about power, respect, persuasion? _____
_____
_____
_____
_____
_____
_____
_____
_____
_____
_____

Prayers, scriptures, poems for court case and legal workings? _____
_____
_____
_____
_____
_____
_____
_____
_____

What are some workings & rituals you use to remove blockages, bad luck, and obstacles in legal workings? _____

_____
_____
_____
_____
_____
_____
_____
_____
_____
_____

What are some workings & rituals you use protect yourself or loved ones from legal harm? _____

_____
_____
_____
_____
_____
_____
_____
_____
_____
_____
_____

What are some workings & rituals you use to gain favor, control, or dominate within the legal system? _____

_____
_____
_____
_____
_____
_____
_____
_____
_____
_____

What are some workings & rituals you use to hide yourself, or shield yourself from the law? _____

_____

_____

_____

_____

_____

_____

_____

_____

What are some workings & rituals you do to ensure success in a legal situation? _____

_____

_____

_____

_____

_____

_____

_____

_____

_____

_____

_____

Court case & legal working oils recipes? _____

_____

_____

_____

_____

_____

_____

_____

_____

_____

Court case & legal working bath recipes? _____
_____
_____
_____
_____
_____
_____
_____
_____
_____

Court case & legal working powder recipes? _____
_____
_____
_____
_____
_____
_____
_____
_____
_____

Court case & legal working candle formulas? _____
_____
_____
_____
_____
_____
_____
_____
_____
_____

Places to bury legal workings? _____
_____
_____
_____
_____
_____
_____
_____
_____

What are some successful legal workings you have performed? _____
_____
_____
_____
_____
_____
_____
_____
_____
_____
_____
_____
_____
_____
_____
_____
_____
_____
_____
_____

23 ACTIVISM/COMMUNITY WORK

Hoodoo is political in its origin. The way we sing is political. The way we speak is political. The way we wear our hair is political. You best believe the spiritual tools of our ancestors are political. At our best, our activism is communal: protect each other, support each other, and be mindful of all types of Black lives. This is basic survival. And on this land, Black survival is political. The activism we do is to wake each other up into remembrance and shine a light on that which seeks to erase us. The blessing of this mantle is the great work and legacies we have available to build upon. When folks say that Hoodoo has no venerable spirits, they quickly disregard our collective ancestors. Many of which are famous activists that devoted their lives to Black survival. When we have communal calls for justice today, we reference them; we lift them, and we continue them.

In the pages ahead, note your knowings & findings in this realm

How do you define community? Is it local? Digital? _____

_____

_____

_____

_____

_____

_____

_____

What dreams and visions do you hold for your community? _____
_____
_____
_____
_____
_____
_____
_____
_____
_____
_____

What are some divination styles or spreads you use to see underlying problems and solutions for communal problems? _____
_____
_____
_____
_____
_____
_____
_____
_____
_____
_____

What are some spiritual and physical omens you recognize that could spell out trouble for your community? _____
_____
_____
_____
_____
_____
_____
_____
_____
_____

What ways do you chose to show up for your community? _____
_____
_____
_____
_____
_____
_____
_____
_____
_____

What ways have elders or ancestors shown up for their community? _____
_____
_____
_____
_____
_____
_____
_____
_____
_____
_____
_____

What community ancestors do you call on in your work? *Activists, thought leaders,*
organizers? _____
_____
_____
_____
_____
_____
_____
_____
_____
_____
_____

Are there any spirit guides or entities you call on for communal workings, activism, or political workings? _____

_____

_____

_____

_____

_____

_____

_____

_____

_____

What day or days of the week, month, and year do you associate with your community?

_____

_____

What numbers do you associate with your community? _____

_____

_____

What colors do you associate with your community? _____

_____

_____

What roots/herbs naturally grow around you bring unity, peace, clear communication?

_____

_____

_____

_____

_____

_____

_____

_____

What roots/herbs in general do you like to use to bring unity, peace, and clear communication? _____

_____

_____

_____

_____

_____

_____

_____

_____

_____

_____

What are some waters you use to heal, bless, or empower your community? _____

_____

_____

What are some dirts you use to heal, bless, or empower your community? _____

_____

_____

What are some incenses you use to heal, bless, or empower your community? _____

_____

_____

What are some crystals you use to heal, bless, or empower your community? _____

_____

_____

What are some symbols you use to heal, bless, or empower your community? _____

_____

_____

What are some animals you use to heal, bless, or empower your community? _____

_____

_____

What are some tools you use to heal, bless, or empower your community? _____
_____
_____

Favorite protest/Black Pride songs? _____
_____
_____
_____
_____
_____
_____
_____
_____

Prayers, scriptures, poems of activism/protest/community? _____
_____
_____
_____
_____
_____
_____
_____
_____
_____

What are some workings & rituals you use to remove blockages, obstacles, or harm in your community? _____
_____
_____
_____
_____
_____
_____
_____
_____

What are some workings & rituals you use to protect your community from threats? __
_____
_____
_____
_____
_____
_____
_____
_____

What are some workings & rituals you use to acknowledge and provide healing to the land of your community? _____
_____
_____
_____
_____
_____
_____
_____
_____

Where do you bury your workings dedicated to your community? _____
_____
_____
_____
_____
_____
_____
_____
_____

What victories have you witnessed in your community work? _____

_____

_____

_____

_____

_____

_____

_____

_____

_____

_____

_____

_____

_____

_____

_____

_____

_____

_____

_____

_____

_____

_____

_____

_____

_____

_____

_____

_____

_____

_____

_____

_____

24 ROOTWORK

Rootwork is the practice of working with the spiritual and medicinal properties of plants for various purposes in the physical realm. Each plant has its own universe of abilities and powers. Herbal magic anthology books often will reduce a single plant to a paragraph, ceasing the conversation with the plant. Leading practitioners to regurgitate the same bullet points about plants like route information. When just beneath the surface exists a world of power, when we allow the plants we work with to tell us how we should work with them. I highly recommend that you work intuitively first when creating relationships with plants. This will allow you to keep an open conversation with the plant. Just because many books and webpages will tell you that bay leaves are great for luck, you may grab a leaf that tells you it should not and will not help you with success. Much of this work is not color by numbers, and what works on one day won't work the next. Relationships reign king. If you work from this direction, you allow yourself to be open to the many discoveries with plants that will never be found in books.

In the pages ahead, note your knowings & findings in this realm. Additional pages can be found on page 239

Plant Name _____

_____

Sacred Names *(any names revealed to you Spirits or the plant itself)* _____

_____

Initial Impressions _____

_____
_____
_____
_____
_____
_____

Personal Connections _____
_____
_____
_____
_____
_____

Familial/Ancestral Connections _____
_____
_____
_____
_____
_____

Religious/Sacred texts mentioning this plant _____
_____
_____
_____
_____
_____

Deities or Spirits affiliated with this plant _____
_____
_____
_____
_____

Instructions or Insight from the Spirit of the Plant _____

_____
_____
_____
_____
_____
_____
_____

Instructions or Insight from your Spiritual Court _____
_____
_____
_____
_____
_____
_____

Instructions or Insight from Teachers/Mentors/Community _____
_____
_____
_____
_____
_____
_____

Personal Learnings/Uses _____
_____
_____
_____
_____
_____

Associated Stories _____
_____
_____
_____
_____

Common Symbolism _____

_____

_____

_____

_____

_____

Workings that incorporate this plant _____

_____

_____

_____

_____

_____

Types of payment for collection *(payment or offerings will vary from plant to plant. It could* *water, smoke, song, public praise, or more. Be ready to listen)* _____

_____

_____

_____

_____

_____

25 ANIMALS

Black cat bone, chicken foot, and gator tooth are tools of the trade for a Hoodoo practitioner. We incorporate animals in our work to honor and utilize their power. Certain animals can lend us great protection, help us dominate an enemy, move through tense situations unscathed, or have the lucky streak we only dreamed of. These powers rely on the knowings of our ancestors held within our families, told in stories, and dictated by Spirits (or the animal themselves). Caution and care must be exercised when incorporating animals into your work. You should start with intuition, and especially in the case of using animals as offerings, seek family, elders, and trusted community members for guidance as to not anger any Spirits or Gods that animal may be sacred to.

In the pages ahead, note your knowings & findings in this realm. Additional pages can be found on page 239

Animal name _____

_____

Sacred names *(any names revealed to you Spirits or the animal itself)* _____

_____

_____

_____

Traits of this animal _____

_____

_____

Initial Impressions _____
_____
_____
_____
_____
_____
_____

Personal connections _____
_____
_____
_____
_____
_____
_____

Familial/Ancestral connections _____
_____
_____
_____
_____
_____
_____

Religious/Sacred texts mentioning this animal _____
_____
_____
_____
_____
_____

Deities or spirits affiliated with this animal _____
_____
_____
_____
_____
_____

Instructions or Insight from the Spirit of the Animal _____

_____

_____

_____

_____

_____

_____

Instructions or Insight from your Spiritual Court _____

_____

_____

_____

_____

_____

_____

Instructions or Insight from Teachers/Mentors/Community _____

_____

_____

_____

_____

_____

_____

Personal Learnings/Uses _____

_____

_____

_____

_____

_____

Associated Stories _____

_____

_____

_____

_____

Common Symbolism _____

_____

_____

_____

_____

_____

Workings that incorporate this animal _____

_____

_____

_____

_____

_____

Types of payment for collection _____

_____

_____

_____

_____

_____

_____

26 WATERS

As humans, water is one of the greatest parents to our existence. As Hoodoos, we have a blessed and complex relationship with her. She carried our ancestors to this land and witnessed every atrocity against us. We've found salvation and baptism in her. She's flooded entire cities and shunned communities to their detriment. Great reverence and respect are demanded of each of us that show up to this work. The forms and functions she can assume are infinite. Depending on where you find her, the time of day you find her, and even the energetic atmosphere around her can influence how water can be used in a working.

In the pages ahead, note your knowings & findings in this realm. Additional pages can be found on page 239

Type of Water _____

_____

Sacred names _____

_____

_____

Initial Impressions _____

_____

_____

_____

_____

_____

Personal Connections _____
_____
_____
_____
_____
_____
_____

Familial/Ancestral Connections _____
_____
_____
_____
_____
_____
_____

Religious/Sacred Texts mentioning this water _____
_____
_____
_____
_____
_____
_____

Deities or spirits affiliated with this water _____
_____
_____
_____
_____
_____
_____

Instructions or Insight from the Spirit of the water _____
_____
_____
_____
_____
_____

Instructions or Insight from your Spiritual Court _____

_____

_____

_____

_____

_____

Instructions or Insight from Teachers/Mentors/Community _____

_____

_____

_____

_____

_____

Personal Learnings/Uses _____

_____

_____

_____

_____

_____

Associated Stories _____

_____

_____

_____

_____

_____

Common Symbolism _____

_____

_____

_____

_____

Workings that incorporate this water _____

_____

_____

_____

_____

_____

Types of payment for collection _____

_____

_____

_____

_____

_____

27 DIRTS

Dirt, simply put, grounds our workings. Incorporating dirt into a working helps give it form in the physical realm. Dirt holds in place the energies of a particular space, arguably stronger than any other element. It's where most of us will return to when our work here is done. And in many creation stories, it's the key element in the spell for human life. All dirt has a different cost, and it depends on the spirits of the place. As with all things, but especially with dirt, there are dangers in taking without paying. Best-case scenario, your working won't yield results. However, in a worst-case scenario, the spirits of the place will come to collect the payment that they see fit.

In the pages ahead, note your knowings & findings in this realm. Additional pages can be found on page 239

Type of dirt _____

_____

Sacred names _____

_____

_____

Initial Impressions _____

_____

_____

_____

_____

_____

Personal Connections _____
_____
_____
_____
_____
_____

Familial/Ancestral Connections _____
_____
_____
_____
_____
_____
_____

Religious/Sacred Texts mentioning this dirt _____
_____
_____
_____
_____
_____
_____

Deities or spirits affiliated with this dirt _____
_____
_____
_____
_____
_____

Instructions or Insight from the Spirits of the Place _____
_____
_____
_____
_____

Instructions or Insight from your Spiritual Court _____

_____

_____

_____

_____

_____

_____

Instructions or Insight from Teachers/Mentors/Community _____

_____

_____

_____

_____

_____

_____

Personal Learnings/Uses _____

_____

_____

_____

_____

_____

Associated Stories _____

_____

_____

_____

_____

_____

Common Symbolism _____

_____

_____

_____

_____

Workings that incorporate this dirt _____
_____
_____
_____
_____
_____

Types of payment for collection _____
_____
_____
_____
_____
_____
_____

28 DEATH WORK

Death rites vary from region to region, family to family, and even person to person in Black America. From the anticipation/preparation, time of death, burial and transition, and mourning/grieving, the underlying rule of the entire process is to respect a loved one's wishes. Rarely will the wishes of a loved one go against the good of the family. If those situations arise, it's best to seek a skilled conjuror, diviner, priest, or death doula to find a remedy. There is great emphasis on how we pay our last respects to our dead, since there are many misfortunes that can occur. Some generational curses that plague families can be traced to an improper burial.

In the pages ahead, note your knowings & findings in this realm

What are your family traditions to prepare for when death is anticipated for a loved one? *(Write down any spiritual and physical things that must be done)* _____
_____
_____
_____
_____
_____
_____
_____
_____
_____
_____

What are your family traditions to prepare when a loved one passes? *(Write down any spiritual and physical things that must be done)* _____

_____

_____

_____

_____

_____

_____

_____

_____

_____

What are the common rituals or rites of passage to ensure a loved one has a safe journey? *(Write down any spiritual and physical things that must be done)* _____

_____

_____

_____

_____

_____

_____

_____

_____

What are your families' burial practices? _____

_____

_____

_____

_____

_____

_____

_____

_____

What is your families' mourning process? grief process? *(if there aren't one in place, write ones you would like to implement)* _____

_____

_____

_____

_____

_____

_____

_____

_____

Are there any superstitions or taboos around death, and funerals in your family? _____

_____

_____

_____

_____

_____

_____

_____

_____

_____

_____

Are there certain rules for burying loved ones in your family? _____

_____

_____

_____

_____

_____

_____

_____

_____

List any common churches, temples, or synagogues your family has had funeral services

_____
_____
_____
_____
_____
_____
_____
_____
_____
_____

List any pastors, priests, shamans, spiritualists, or death doulas that have helped family members in the death process _____

_____
_____
_____
_____
_____
_____
_____
_____
_____
_____
_____

29 CEMETERY WORK

Many types of work can be done in a cemetery. Stereotypically, folks solely think of curses and hexes when it comes to cemetery work. But everything from cleansing, love, protection, money, and healing work can be done in a cemetery. It just requires the right perspective (*and the right precautions*). The first type of cemetery spirits you should work with are YOUR OWN. As is constantly stressed, and reiterated here as well, working with your personal ancestors first will save you many dangers and messes that can happen with in cemetery work. When you feel ready to move beyond working with solely your ancestors, it is highly suggested you build an actual relationship with a cemetery before decide to do work. If there is a community group that cleans up and looks after the cemetery, see if you can join. If this isn't an ancestral cemetery to you, research who is buried there, and what they meant to the surrounding community. Even the slightest effort of getting to know a cemetery will help you tremendously before you beginning to do work.

In the pages ahead, note your knowings & findings in this realm

What cemeteries are attributed to your family? (*Include name and location*) _____
_____
_____
_____
_____
_____
_____

What cemeteries have you developed relationship to outside of your family? _____

_____

_____

_____

_____

_____

Are there any divinations styles, spreads, tools, or signs you seek for permission to enter a cemetery? _____

_____

_____

_____

_____

_____

_____

_____

_____

What are your practices for entering a cemetery safely? _____

_____

_____

_____

_____

Acceptable forms of payment for items sourced from your cemeteries? _____

_____

_____

_____

_____

_____

Acceptable forms of payment for workings done in your cemeteries? _____
_____
_____
_____
_____
_____
_____

List any ancestors you commonly work with at the cemetery, and the types of workings you go to them for? _____
_____
_____
_____
_____
_____
_____
_____
_____
_____

List any non-ancestral spirits you work with at the cemetery, and the types of workings you go to them for? _____
_____
_____
_____
_____
_____
_____
_____
_____
_____

List any spirit guides or entities you use in your cemetery work? _____
_____
_____

_____
_____
_____
_____
_____
_____
_____
_____

What are your practices for leaving a cemetery safely? _____

_____
_____
_____
_____

Dangers, warnings, taboos about working in the cemetery? _____

_____
_____
_____
_____

30 GHOSTS, HAGS, & HAINTS

These types of spirits come with the territory of Hoodoo. Lost souls, dark spirits, or fragments of spirits exist in every culture. In America, there are all sorts of unrecognized pain and traumas in the land that seek to wreak havoc in our lives. Sometimes they're the result of a spiritual attack from another practitioner. Other times they just exist in a space you're in. Many of these spirits gain entry in our lives through a crack of fear in our foundation. They can exploit our insecurities and compel us to act out their desires through whispered thoughts. And some simply just want to feast on our good energy. It is necessary to be mindful of these spirits, but not to be fearful in any form that would give them your power. Command your victory in any encounters of negative spirits, and see it through.

In the pages ahead, note your knowings & findings in this realm. Additional pages can be found on page 239

Name of Entity _____

_____

Alternative or Specific names _____

_____

_____

What feeds them? _____

_____

_____

_____

How you recognize them? _____
_____
_____
_____
_____
_____
_____

Dangers, powers, abilities? _____
_____
_____
_____
_____
_____

Memorable encounters _____
_____
_____
_____
_____
_____
_____
_____
_____
_____
_____

How to remove/send it away _____
_____
_____
_____
_____
_____

Associated stories _____
_____
_____
_____
_____
_____
_____
_____

Lessons learned from this entity _____
_____
_____
_____
_____
_____
_____
_____
_____
_____
_____

31 ANGELS, SAINTS, & SPIRIT GUIDES

Conjuring with various spirits can be complex work. Many things can go right, and many (many) things can go wrong. Before engaging in work with spirits outside of your ancestry, it is suggested you develop a strong sense of discernment. This can be practiced and exercised while working with your ancestors. Ask questions frequently to confirm their presence, and to ensure your understanding of their messages to you. When you feel comfortable discerning, remain in the habit of asking a Spirit their name when you recognize its presence. Even when a spirit tells you their name, be aware that some spirits can lie. But with discernment, you may feel the disingenuousness in their reply. Most importantly of all work with spirits, NEVER make an offer you can't uphold. Even if it's something as small as 3 pennies, make sure to give those three pennies to that spirit. The offended spirit could be inclined to take $300 in exchange for your negligence, or worse. Additionally, it is never wise to ask a spirit "What do you want? I'll give you anything". Desperation should be fully extinguished when entering spiritual work. Think practically.

In the pages ahead, note your knowings & findings in this realm. Additional pages can be found on page 239

Name of Spirit _____

_____

Sacred names _____

_____

_____

Abilities, powers, knowledges? _____

_____

_____

_____

_____

_____

_____

How to conjure them? _____

_____

_____

_____

_____

_____

How you recognize their presence? _____

_____

_____

_____

_____

_____

Offerings they tend to like? _____

_____

_____

_____

_____

_____

Workings that incorporate them? _____

_____

_____

_____

_____

_____
_____
_____
_____
_____
_____
_____
_____

Memorable Encounters _____
_____
_____
_____
_____
_____

How to dismiss/send away? _____
_____
_____
_____
_____
_____

Associated stories _____
_____
_____
_____
_____
_____
_____
_____
_____
_____

Lessons from this spirit? _____

_____

_____

_____

_____

_____

_____

_____

_____

_____

_____

_____

32 BABIES

Many critical keys to our culture's survival were and are currently held in the hands of Black midwives and doulas. They usher in new life into the physical realm and ensure safety and good health of the child and the mother. The work of birthing touches on healing, prosperity, protection, divination, cleansing, and many other realms. Much of that work MUST be passed down directly from practitioner to practitioner. Not all conjurors and Hoodoo practitioners will be called to work with babies and birthing. And that's okay. You can still add to this section because you'll never know when you (or a future descendant) will urgently need this information.

In the pages ahead, note your knowings & findings in this realm

Dream symbolisms related to babies (*Write down any common symbolism that if seen in a dream could mean a baby's arrival, a warning, or a specific message about a baby.*) _____

_____

_____

_____

_____

_____

_____

_____

_____

_____

Write any omens you recognize to being warnings about a baby? _____

_____

_____

_____

_____

_____

_____

Divination symbolisms related to babies. (*Write down any cards or tools that if seen during a reading could mean a baby's arrival, a warning, or a specific message about a baby.*) _____

_____

_____

_____

_____

_____

_____

_____

_____

_____

What ancestors do you have that were midwives, doulas, doctors, or great mothers of the family? _____

_____

_____

_____

_____

_____

_____

_____

_____

What living folks do you have in your family that are midwives, doulas, doctors, or great mothers of the family? _____

_____

_____

_____

_____

_____

Any spirit guides or entities you work with to ensure babies arrive safely into the physical realm? _____

_____

_____

_____

_____

_____

_____

_____

_____

What roots and herbs naturally ground around you that promote fertility and healthy pregnancy? _____

_____

_____

_____

_____

_____

_____

_____

What roots and herbs do you like to use in general that promote fertility and healthy pregnancy? _____

_____

_____

_____

_____

_____

_____

_____

_____

_____

What waters do you use or work with to promote fertility and healthy pregnancy? _____

_____

_____

What dirts do you use or work with to promote fertility and healthy pregnancy? _____

_____

_____

What incense do you use or work with to promote fertility and healthy pregnancy? ____

_____

_____

What crystals do you use or work with to promote fertility and healthy pregnancy? ____

_____

_____

What symbols do you use or work with to promote fertility and healthy pregnancy? ____

_____

_____

What animals do you use or work with to promote fertility and healthy pregnancy? ____

_____

_____

What tools do you use or work with to promote fertility and healthy pregnancy? _____
_____
_____

What songs do you use or work with to promote fertility and healthy pregnancy? _____
_____
_____
_____
_____
_____
_____
_____
_____

Prayers, scriptures, poems for fertility and pregnancy? _____
_____
_____
_____
_____
_____
_____
_____
_____

What are some workings & rituals you use to remove blockages to those seeking to have a safe and successful pregnancy? _____
_____
_____
_____
_____
_____
_____

What are some workings & protections you use to ensure the baby has a healthy arrival?

_____
_____
_____
_____
_____
_____
_____
_____

What are some workings & rituals you do to ensure the baby is blessed? _____

_____
_____
_____
_____
_____
_____
_____
_____

Fertility oil recipes? _____

_____
_____
_____
_____
_____
_____

Fertility bath recipes? _____

_____
_____
_____
_____
_____
_____

Fertility powder recipes? _____
_____
_____
_____
_____
_____
_____

Fertility candle formulas? _____
_____
_____
_____
_____
_____
_____

Places to sew fertility workings _____
_____
_____
_____
_____
_____
_____

What are some successful births you have had a hand in, physically or spiritually? _____

_____

_____

_____

_____

_____

_____

_____

_____

_____

_____

_____

_____

_____

_____

_____

_____

_____

_____

_____

_____

_____

_____

_____

_____

_____

_____

_____

_____

33 NOTES FOR FUTURE GENERATIONS

If the day should come that you decide to gift this book to a descendant of yours, what words of wisdom would you want to bestow unto them?

GLOSSARY

- Ancestors: Deceased loved ones within your family that have gone through the afterlife process(s) to become venerated and connect with living descendants.

- Angels: A group of ordained Spirits by God that all humans have access to call upon for various types of help and goals.

- Cemetery: A burial site owned by a city, government organization, nonprofit organization, family, or other group. Depending on ownership, someone may or may not look after these burial sites.

- Conjure: The practice of drawing forth and working with spirits to produce desired goals in the physical realm. In the South, Conjure is sometimes synonymous with Hoodoo and Rootwork. The act of conjuration spans various magical traditions and systems.

- Elder: A living family member or community member of an older generation.

- Graveyard: A burial site near and connected to a church. These will often be more maintained, regulated, and looked after by church personnel.

- Hag: A type of negative entity that plagues people at night, sitting on top of their chest, stealing their breath and energy as they sleep.

- Haint/Haunt: A dark type of ghost, or fragment of a Spirit that seeks to plague people, especially at night, feeding off fear.

- Hoodoo: An African American spiritual practice, forged from the merging of African cultures (Kongo, Yoruba, Ewe, Fon, Bantu, Igbo) into enslavement in America.

- Left-Handed Work: A synonymous term to describe curses, hexes, and baneful magic.

- Magic: The power of creating a change in one's reality by supernatural means.

- Rootwork: The African-American tradition of working with the spiritual or medicinal properties of plants to product healing effects. Rootwork can sometimes be synonymous with Hoodoo and Conjure. In some contexts and regions, Rootwork strictly means someone who works with the medicinal properties of plants.

- Saints: People who, in death, are elevated to a status of high virtue, allowing them to help the living in the areas of life in which they excelled.

- Spirit Court: The collective group of Ancestors, Spirit Guides, Angels, etc. that watch over a person.

- Spirit Guides: Spirits that may or may not be ancestral, that seek to help a person. This help may be for a certain period of time, or all throughout their life, to accomplish certain tasks and goals.

- Taboo: A restriction or forbidden task someone is not allowed to do based on spiritual concerns. Taboos are usually determined and governed by a Spirit or authoritative spiritual figure as a means to protect someone from danger.

- Veneration: The act of paying high honor and respect to an Ancestor, Spirit, or Deity. Not to be confused with worship or praise, veneration can help elevate Spirits.

- Working: An often-coded way to describe a spell or ritual. A 'working' can sometimes describe a more labor-intensive type of spell or ritual.

WORKS REFERENCED

Chesnutt, Charles W. The Conjure Woman. Flame Tree 451, 2023.

Hazzard-Donald, Katrina. Mojo Workin': The Old African American Hoodoo System. University of Illinois Press, 2013.

Hurston, Zora Neale. Mules and Men. Harper & Row, 1990.

Johnson, F. Roy. The Fabled Doctor Jim Jordan: A Story of Conjure. N.C., 1968.

Bae, Juju. A Little Juju Podcast, 2018.

LEE, MICHELE ELIZABETH. Working the Roots: Over 400 Years of Traditional African American Healing. WADASTICK, 2017.

McQuillar, Tayannah Lee. Rootwork: Using the Folk Magick of Black America for Love, Money, and Success. Simon & Schuster, 2003.

Raboteau, Albert J. Slave Religion: The "Invisible Institution" in the Antebellum South. Oxford University Press, 2004.

Rue, Mama. Mama Rue's Ancestral Musings Podcast, 2020.

Teish, Luisah. Jambalya: The Natural Woman's Book of Personal Charms and Practical Rituals. HarperCollins, 2021.

Additional printable pages for documentation can be found at
www.TheHoodooHandbook.com/downloads

Or scan this QR code for free access to the .pdf downloads

ABOUT THE AUTHOR

James E. Stewart IV is a Hoodoo practitioner, Rootworker, and Conjuror from Durham, NC. He has learned from various teachers, elders, & the spiritual community. He is the owner & operator of Conjure Cleaning, and spiritual home cleansing company.

www.ingramcontent.com/pod-product-compliance
Lightning Source LLC
Chambersburg PA
CBHW080838120626
46553CB00009B/2480